D1154181

THE MORAL TROLLOPE

By

Ruth apRoberts

OHIO UNIVERSITY PRESS 1971

©Ruth apRoberts 1971
Printed by offset and bound in the United States of America
for Ohio University Press, Athens, Ohio
by The Watkins Printing Co.
LC 75-141383
ISBN 8214-0089-4

To
MY FAMILY

ACKNOWLEDGEMENTS

Parts of this book have appeared in slightly different form in the following articles: "Trollope Empiricus," *Victorian Newsletter* (Autumn, 1968); "Anthony Trollope: or, the Man with no Style at All," *Victorian Newsletter* (Spring, 1969), "Trollope's One World," *The South Atlantic Quarterly* (Autumn, 1969); "Trollope's Casuistry," *Novel* (Autumn, 1969).

CONTENTS

Chapter I

THE ESSENTIAL NOVELIST

How seldom it is that theories stand the wear and tear of
practice!

TROLLOPE, IN *Thackeray*

THERE is something of a mystery in the case of Anthony
Trollope. His novels constitute a phenomenon of acknowledged success and importance, but still go largely
unexplained. Accepted, admired, and—above all—*read*, read
widely and in depth (and they are one hundred and nine
volumes deep), by the sort of people who like to be able to
explain things to themselves, people whom you can hardly
call naïve, the novels have nevertheless not yet earned the
dignity of a rationale. Trollope himself defended 'English
Prose Fiction as a Rational Amusement,'[1] and we might try
to do the same by him. Not that we can pluck out the heart
of his mystery, but we might be able to circumscribe, define,
and perhaps reduce the mystery to a certain extent. I think
the chances of some success are better now than they were;
the inadequacies of our older theories of fiction have become
embarrassing, and there have been many new openings made,
and castings about for more serviceable aesthetics of fiction.
Our old ones were tailored to Flaubert and James and Joyce.
They have been occasionally useful but more often worse than
useless for Cervantes, for Tolstoi, for Fielding, Sterne, Jane
Austen, Scott, Thackeray and Trollope. Of all English
novelists Trollope seems to be the perfect example of the kind
least served by our old theories; and for this very reason, to
come to grips with his work may help us towards a new and
more workable theory. In what way do his novels succeed for
reasons that James, or Lubbock, or Leavis, do not recognise?
By trying to answer this, we may do Trollope a service, and at

11

the same time discover some things hitherto neglected in the study of the novel as genre.

The precise reasons for the critical neglect of Trollope are worth discussing. He seems, first, to have a way of teasing you out of thought. You may start a Trollope novel with a critical curiosity; you want to know just what it is he does, and how he does it, and then—fatally—you slip into the posture of consumer rather than critic. This does not happen to all readers, but it does happen to many rather well qualified ones. The charming and modest statement of Nathaniel Hawthorne is often quoted, but it needs to be quoted once more here:

> If I were to meet with such books as mine by another writer, I don't believe I should be able to get through them. Have you ever read the novels of Anthony Trollope? They precisely suit my taste.[2]

And then there is a little story told by J. I. M. Stewart about Yeats and *Ulysses*.

> Yeats declared *Ulysses* to be a mad book, later pronounced it a work of genius surpassing in intensity any novel of its time, and finally [was] unable to finish it so that he found himself reading Trollope instead.[3]

Trollope novels often so seem to open themselves, as it were. They may precisely suit our taste, but we are at a loss to say why. But this readableness, so well attested, must, after all, be an essential virtue of fiction. Whatever the novel is, this quality must be one of its strongest points, and readable novels, one might think, should be a defensible kind.

There has been a considerable body of writing about Trollope, certainly. It is mostly of two sorts, neither of which really comes to terms with him as an artist. The first is the broad survey; because his output is so large and so various, the surveys are a great help towards giving us a sense of his accomplishment. Michael Sadleir and Bradford A. Booth have been invaluable in this way, classifying Trollope's output, characterising the categories, and making relative evaluations. The other sort of writing is the short appreciative essay, which tends to be graceful and charming. Both the surveyors and the appreciators—and their names make an illustrious list— record occasional fine insights; there are many leads to be found in these writings which would take us far towards a useful analysis. But these appreciators, when they write about Trollope, write more as enthusiasts than as critics. We know the history of Jane Austen criticism, and the effect of cultism: the Jane-ites did for a time seriously impede the study of Jane Austen's novels. The Trollopians, happy band though they are, had better come into the forum and think tough.

Trollopian cultism has been persistent, I think, for certain reasons having to do with the nature of its leader, Michael Sadleir. Of course Trollope studies owe him an incalculable debt: his *Trollope: A Bibliography* is not only a model of its kind but also a blessed head start to all students of Trollope, and his *Trollope: A Commentary* is a mine of both information and insight. But there are nevertheless qualities in Sadleir's work that have vitiated the study of Trollope. Sadleir is a fine example of the bibliophile and dilettante, and no one wants to do without the type; but he is so good at being what he is that he has set the key for too much writing about Trollope. His delighted connoisseurship impedes actual analysis. In effect, however much Sadleir actually admires Trollope, he has a basically condescending attitude.

This has not gone altogether unremarked. Paul Elmer More cried about it in the wilderness at the time the Sadleir *Commentary* was published. What he had to say then in 1928 seems very much to the point right now.[4] The *Commentary* is 'an excellent book in the main, broadly informative, richly documented, often finely critical.' But, says More, although it is 'intended to be laudatory, yet [it has] that current note of apology which so frequently annoys me in those who profess themselves Trollopians.' Sadleir 'thinks it necessary to

apologise for him as intellectually without ideas and imagi-
natively without wings,' and More asserts that the fault
springs from the inadequacy of the current theories of art,
which lead Sadleir to 'belittle critically what instinctively he
admires.' More himself was so violently at odds with the
Jamesian and Joycean aesthetic of his time, that his negative
criticism is often too splenetic for us. But where he praises
he praises well, and his own aesthetic enables him to apprehend
the particular values in Trollope's art. He has the wit to see
through Trollope's way of self-deprecation that has taken in
so many.

> If any novelist ever wove his plots with a definite idea before
> him about the meaning of life in general, it was this same
> 'unideaed' Trollope; he is as clear in his conception of human
> destiny as George Eliot, and if anything truer to the facts.

To deny Trollope ideas 'is a slander upon the novelist and an
insult to his devoted readers.' More insists on the relation
between ethics and art, and considers that Trollope relates
them well. He appreciates how Trollope is able to avoid the
strain of eighteenth-century sentimental morality that sur-
vives in Thackeray. He insists that Trollope's art is not at all
weakened by authorial comment but positively *enhanced*.
And he reveres Trollope, not only for the 'understanding of
the individual human heart,' but also for his 'feeling for the
vast integrity of civilisation.' All these things have been hard
for us to appreciate under the early-twentieth-century critical
Establishment. More could do so because of his own bias,
which seemed idiosyncratic in his time but may seem less so
now. As I hope to show, Trollope stands in the stream of
liberal humanism that is More's great critical theme; and
More's 'Demon of the Absolute' is Trollope's enemy too.

But let us look now more closely at the limitations of this
early-twentieth-century critical Establishment. If Sadleir
and other critics 'belittle critically what instinctively they
admire,' just what are the reasons for the belittlement?
Philip Rahv, in 'Fiction and the Criticism of Fiction,'[5] a

good instance of a new kind of thinking about the novel, explains that the trouble lies in what has been an effort 'to deduce a prosaics from a poetics.' The effort to apply the criteria of poetry to fiction has saddled us with—he says—three critical biases, which have made us swerve off in various wrong directions.

The first on Rahv's list is our penchant for searching out fiction for symbol, allegory and myth. Indubitably, some fiction needs this kind of scrutiny: you cannot begin to grasp *Ulysses* without an appreciation of its mythic pattern. And there is no doubt that Dickens has a tendency to symbols. That fog in *Bleak House* is indeed more than an ordinary London meteorological variation. But the trouble is, as Rahv says, that the search for symbols and so on 'debilitates the critical mind.' No one who is intellectually responsible is unaware of the foolish excesses of this kind of thing. And these excesses spring from the misdirected effort of applying poetic method to prose. Another misdirection comes from taking style to be the essential activity of fiction, Rahv says. And he makes an example of John Crowe Ransom 'proving' that Jane Austen is greater than Tolstoi, on the basis of little snippets from each. One may sympathise with Ransom: it is desirable to argue from an exhibit and one cannot quote a whole novel. But Rahv's objection stands. Style in fiction must hold a different place from what it does in poetry. Speed-reading is conceivably legitimate, even desirable, for *Clarissa Harlowe*, but it is no more proper for *Paradise Lost* than for *The Skylark*. Both symbolic explication and *stylism*, then, are overworked for fiction; and the third overworked approach, says Rahv, is *technicism*. We have put far too much emphasis on technique. Formalist analysis of novels can discover a great deal to us, and has, and it can at the same time bypass some essential and characteristic fortes of the genre.

Trollope makes a good test case for Rahv's anti-poetics position. He is the least symbolic of novelists; he is least of a 'stylist'; and he exhibits little of those technical excellences the formalists admire beyond all else. I should like to suggest that on each of these counts he is all the more the artist of the novel proper, and we can characterise his particular art on each count.

Let us take him first as a non-symbolist. There are certainly symbols in Trollope's work, as there are in any phase of human life. But I think it can be said he is as little symbolic as an artist in words can be. The symbols we find in Trollope are symbols for his characters rather than for us. Certainly, his people make use of non-verbal communication. When Will Belton the farmer sends a courting present to Clara Amedroz, he makes his point eloquently. The present is, of all things, a cow. A real cow, particularly real. And the warm, pretty, milky thing is a good token of the earthiness of Will's real passion, clearly contrasted to the frigidity of Clara's other suitor, Captain Aylmer. The Captain's tepid and vacillating courtship, his avoidance of physical contact, and his subservience to his mother, all perfectly indicate his sexual inadequacy. Will is a little short on verbal eloquence and finds the cow an effective solution to the communication problem. The cow speaks to Clara; but he, Trollope, speaks to us in words. He glories in his own verbalism. His forte is the de-symbolising of things for us, clear, terse verbal exposition, often so witty that we hardly realise we have apprehended a subtle psychological fact. Joseph E. Baker quotes a good example of this in a stout-hearted and useful attempt to pin down Trollope's quality. He calls it 'Trollope's Third Dimension'[6] and the passage he quotes tells us something of the Countess de Courcy. She is the mother of three daughters whose marriage prospects are not bright; and she has just heard of the engagement of her acquaintance, young Lily Dale.

> 'I dare say it will come to nothing,' said the countess, who liked to hear of girls being engaged and then losing their proposed husbands. She did not know she liked it, but she

did; and already had pleasure in anticipating poor Lily's discomfiture (*The Small House at Allington*, XVII).*

Surely there is something here that we can all recognise as the way a human being sometimes functions; and we may well recognise we have never had it anatomised before. Nothing is suggested, or connoted, or invoked, or adumbrated. It is precise descriptive analysis, verbal, plain and unequivocally clear. It may be that Trollope's 'third dimension,' his mysterious power, is in fact plain non-metaphoric exposition. This is a possible excellence in fiction that we are not much used to respecting or analysing. Examples are everywhere in Trollope's work. Take, for instance, the occasion of an argument between Archdeacon Grantly and his wife. The Archdeacon thought, at such times, 'that his wife took an unfair advantage of him by keeping her temper' (*Last Chronicle,* LVI). We are inclined to enjoy these things, and ticket them as merely funny. But they are not *mere* at all. They are very important, and they are Trollope's quality, because they are really brilliant discoveries in psychology, recorded in baldest terms. We experience the joy of discovery in these analytical statements, that are witty just because they are both terse and true.

His method of descriptive analysis of the workings of men and women leaves no room for the novelistic set piece of 'description.' The early *Macdermots of Ballycloran* comes closest to it, perhaps: in it, Trollope does set a scene of the decay and ruin of real estate, for the playing out of a tragic story of the decay and ruin of a family. But in the main body of his work, this is not his way. There are virtually no atmospheric descriptions and no pathetic fallacies. He gives you a

*In referring to Trollope's novels I give only the chapter number because there are so many editions and they lack standardisation. Where the chapter numbering varies I follow the practice of W. G. and J. T. Gerould's *Guide to Trollope*, Princeton University Press, Princeton and Oxford University Press, London, 1948. (For instance, for *The American Senator*, I follow the one-volume edition, chapter numbers I to LXXX, instead of the three-volume edition in which each volume has separate numbering. There is a conversion table in the Gerould Guide, p. xxiii.)

bald circumstantial description of a country house or a village because you have to know the geography to understand the action. Or he describes the furnishings of Madame Max Goesler's apartment because it helps to explain her character and her attractiveness. There is an interesting case in a late novel, *An Eye for an Eye,* where there is indeed a vivid description that, if excised, would seem a set piece of fine atmospheric or poetic writing. But in context it has a more special function. Most of the novel is set in Ireland, and to a certain point the 'local colour' Trollope gives us is quite prosaic; there is excellent Irish dialect, and the vivid character of the priest, and these are necessary parts of the story. And then in a critical chapter Fred Neville the hero must climb the hill to face the consequence of his action, to face the girl he has made pregnant, and her mother, who has been his friend; circumstances are such that he is convinced he cannot make amends by marrying the girl. He is a seducer, but not a heartless one. He loathes himself now, and as he slowly climbs the hill to the girl's house, Trollope shows us Fred's view of the landscape. It is a bleak Irish scene: wretched huts more fit for animals than men, on barren rocky ground, a desolate and blasted land. But this landscape is there because it demonstrates the hero's state of mind: it is plainly a *paysage intérieure.* In the earlier days of the wooing and winning these same hills were not desolate. Fred, in the midst of his self-loathing, finds that everything has turned weary, stale, flat and unprofitable.

In this way, what description there is in Trollope is directly functional as exposition. No scene is written to put us in a mood, as music can; no coiling ubiquitous fog alerts us to a theme; no dust-heap suggests the corrupting power of riches. No sacred number suggests to us the Trinity or the Stations of the Cross. Trollope is, of all writers, the least legitimate ground for the search for symbols.

But sometimes it seems as though no piece of literature is sacred. I mean, of course, that none can be safely left as secular. One critic has at last turned exegetically on Anthony Trollope: the twelve bedesmen in *The Warden,* by reason of their twelveness, are said to suggest Christian allegory.[7] The number is really just about as significant as eggs. Neither Christ nor the English have been strong for the metric system, and a dozen apostles, or a dozen eggs, or a dozen bedesmen are all so numbered just because a dozen is felt to be a round number. The critic who sees allegory in *The Warden* ends by embarrassing even himself. He pictures Mr. Harding's 'cello, and sees 'the cross formed by the bow upon the string,' and then he has to say 'But surely this is going too far.' It is. At least it has not often been necessary to combat this sort of thing in Trollope criticism. He has protected himself pretty well by the nature of his realism. His own characters speak out against allegoresis, by their clear insistence on their realness, being people and not symbols. There may be archetypal patterns in Trollope but they are not worth looking for. In the main, this is so obvious one has not been obliged to say it.

So much for Rahv's first count, the count of symbolism. On his second count, stylism, there is more to say, and some of it has recently been said, and said well. Already there is a new view of Trollope's style that stands in declared opposition to the old stylism Rahv deplores, and the new view indicates the trend both in Trollope studies and in critical theory. The main traditional pronouncement used to be that Trollope's style is plain, dull, and flat. Lord David Cecil goes so far as to say it is *nothing.* Trollope has *no style.*[8] And of course this is taken to be a lack, a fault, a failing. Philip Rahv would invite us to a careful consideration of this. He reminds us that Balzac, Stendhal, and Dostoevski are all indifferent stylists, and he proposes that evaluation of novels on the basis of style is, then, hardly defensible. Of course, just as some novels have their being in the symbolic mode, so there are also some that live on style. Flaubert is the great exemplar: no one who has seen the transcriptions of the manuscripts of *Madame Bovary* with their multitudinous revisions can think of

Flaubert's text as anything less careful than poetry. It is his own particular marvel that he combines the more usual merits of fiction with a prose where every cadence is exquisite and every *mot* is *juste*.

But novelists do not typically use words as poets do. There is only one novel made up out of words in the poet's way: it is *Finnegans Wake*, and what *Finnegans Wake* lacks are those things that are generally felt to be proper to novels. The poem, asserts Rahv, is organised according to the structure of language, while the novel is organised according to the structure of the reality portrayed. This is why, he declares, the novel translates so well. A 'jewelled' style is positively a disadvantage to the novelist; for novels are 'not composed of words. They are composed of scenes, actions, *stuff*, and people.' The critic's function, then, is most properly to investigate the translatable qualities of fiction.

But for now, what of Trollope's English? The old objections to his *nothing* style have recently been rejected. The most thoroughgoing rejection is David Aitkin's 'A Kind of Felicity,' modestly subtitled 'Some Notes about Trollope's Style.'[9] He urges this point:

> It is to the matter of his books—their characters and stories, and their freight of moral implication—that he wants his audience to pay attention, not to the manner. . . . He is always a little contemptuous of the self-conscious literary artist, the 'man who thinks much of his words as he writes' (*Autobiography*, pp. 148–149). 'Style is to the writer,—not the wares which he has to take to market, but the vehicle in which they may be carried' (*Duke's Children*, xxvi).

Aitkin demonstrates the apparent effortless simplicity of the writing, and the informality of the vocabulary, and the occasional spells of formal or ponderous words which were partly the doubtful humour of the time, partly Trollope's own little game. These spells of 'officialese,' as Bradford A. Booth called it, may function, Aitkin suggests, to 'alter the light in which we see familiar human problems.' The sentences are remarkably simple in structure, and often elegant; and Aitkin reminds us of Trollope's avowed care that he 'so train his ear that he shall be able to weigh the rhythm of every word as it falls from his pen.'[10] No jarring sound, that is, may be allowed to distract from the matter. In wit, in 'speed and tautness,' he is often like Jane Austen. The tone is intimate, and there is 'the flavour of easy talk.' His imagery is occasionally brilliant: Aitkin quotes an example from the tersely drawn character of Lord Fawn:

> Within the short straight grooves of Lord Fawn's intellect the remembrance of this supposed wrong was always running up and down, renewing its own soreness (*Eustace Diamonds*, XVI).

But on the whole, Aitkin insists, imagery is 'rather unimportant in the general scheme of his art.' Many of his images are repeated so often, and are so commonplace anyway—I would add to Aitkin's comment—that they simply do not function as images; the world is one's oyster, the beautiful woman is the candle to the moth, people row in the same boat, and so on. I might further add that this is a way Chaucer also had, in his stories—to draw on the common stock of conventional figures of speech. Such images are hardly what we are used to calling poetic, as all they do is maintain an air of comfortable ordinariness between teller and reader. And certainly the sum of all these things Aitkin remarks indicates a style that pointedly refuses to call attention to itself. Trollope scorns the novelist 'who thinks much of his words as he writes.' As though to support Philip Rahv, Trollope himself makes clear that he is speaking of fiction when he says this; he himself is quite clear that the case of poetry is altogether different.[11]

Geoffrey Tillotson, in a little essay called 'Trollope's Style,'[12] makes a general declaration: Trollope 'stands firmly among the dozen or so giants of English fiction,' and yet criticism strangely neglects him. Tillotson feels the time is ripe for analysis of Trollope, and he himself makes an opening into this problem of style. He acclaims Trollope's style for its lack

of pretensions, and says, 'It reveals its honesty in its pre-
ference for monosyllables. . . . It abhors the high-sounding,'
but does not abhor grace. 'Rather it is the style of one who
knows how best to sustain grace *without its seeming too much a
thing of art*. . . . It is a style for all purposes, being capable
of handling the trivial and commonplace, and also the noble
and splendid—it can indeed also handle the complicated
when used by one who, like Trollope, *always masters complexity* so that it is reduced to its elements' (my italics).

Can it be we have been so attuned to poetic style that we
have been unable to appreciate an achievement in discursive
statement, in prose? So often Trollope's rather tongue-in-
cheek comments on his methods have been taken at face
value; we have believed his work is like that of the shoemaker he is forever comparing himself to, when all he intends
is to deflate the waiting-for-inspiration theory of composition,
and to recommend a valiant discipline. Because his prose is
easy to read, and because it was produced on time, we think
it must have been easy to write. It is so simple and so clear
that we incline to slight it. Of course that is just what he
aimed at. He *masters complexity*; he makes us forget the
words while we apprehend effortlessly the most tenuous
delicacies of nuance in psychology, or social situations of the
most extreme complexity. We grasp these and then cheat him
of his praise, for he distracts us from the manner with his
matter. It is a technique he practised tirelessly; every day he
whittled and sharpened it. One can still see the journeyman in
The Warden and *Barchester Towers*; here is manner and arch-
ness and uncertainty, at times. But the later writing hardly
ever falters in its efficiency. Trollope himself says, in the
terms of the latest technology of his day, 'The language used
should be as ready and as *efficient* a conductor of the mind of
the writer to the mind of the reader as is the electric spark
which passes from one battery to another.'[13] And again, *lucid*,
or the intensive *pellucid*, is the word he uses most often to
describe the best way for the novelist to write. *Lucid*. Let

the medium be as glass, through which everything shows clear. Let the medium be as *nothing*. Trollope, says Lord David Cecil, has *no style*.

Tillotson says Trollope's style is like Dr. Johnson's. And he thinks that Dr. Johnson, much as he deprecated novels, would have approved of Trollope's. I think so too. Trollope does not offend in the way Johnson considered his contemporaries in the novel to offend. Johnson and Trollope have a similar sense of the decorous; they are both devoted conventional Anglicans, both great moralists; they both combine a grand and wide humour with a sympathetic sense of the tragic in life, and a sense of the doubleness of things. (They *did* have that little tiff, when the young Trollope threw Johnson's *Lives* out the window for 'sneering' at *Lycidas*.)[14] W. P. Ker noted the likeness between Johnson and Trollope a long time ago, observing by the way that Johnson's 'A man may write at any time if he will set himself doggedly to it,' is very close to the message of Trollope's *Autobiography*, and it is not only an attitude to art but also to life.[15] 'It's dogged as does it,' is the sole theme of comfort to Josiah Crawley in his hour of agony in *The Last Chronicle*. Johnson and Trollope have indeed very much in common, in their grand basic moral attitudes. Not so much in style, I think. A great Lexicographer can never be so unselfconscious about words as to write as plain as Trollope. Johnson was too learned, too much the Great Cham, to let the manner go and give himself up utterly to the matter. Aitkin also rejects the comparison to Johnson, and he proposes Macaulay instead. And there is some point in this, too, for both Macaulay and Trollope are remarkable for beautiful clarity. Indeed, Trollope credits Macaulay with having simplified English sentence structure 'with his multiplicity of divisions.'[16] But if we look to the recent fine analysis of Macaulay's style by William Madden, as *oratorical*, as *judicious*, as *histrionic*,[17] we are only helped to define Trollope's as private and intimate rather than oratorical, qualified and relativistic rather than judicious, relaxed and frank rather than histrionic. Actually, Trollope himself tells us where to look; he tells us who his master is.

> I hold that gentleman to be the best dressed whose dress no one observes. I am not sure but that the same may be said of an author's written language. Only, where shall we find an example of such perfection? Always easy, always lucid, always correct, we may find them; but who is the writer, easy, lucid and correct, who has not impregnated his writing with something of the personal flavour we call mannerism? To speak of authors well-known to all readers—Does not *The Rambler* taste of Johnson; *The Decline and Fall*, of Gibbon; . . . *The History of England*, of Macaulay . . .? I have sometimes thought that Swift has been nearest to the mark of any —writing English and not writing Swift.[18]

That is what Trollope aimed at—the style so *lucid* that it does not show at all, writing which refuses attention to the words. By reason of this, 'the reality portrayed,' the *stuff* of the novel, is so much more insistently itself. Surely *Gulliver* is remarkably prosaic, bald, clean of rhetoric, and translatable. And surely it is because of this deliberate unremarkableness that Swift can manipulate so well the facets of his reality, and impose *his* extraordinary vision.

In the passage on Swift Trollope goes on to say,

> But I doubt whether an accurate observer would not trace even here the 'mark of the beast.' Thackeray [who is the occasion of these remarks], too, has a strong flavour of Thackeray.

It seems for a minute here that style is something like original sin—the mark of the beast, indeed! One would like to tell Philip Rahv about it. We might object to Trollope's comment on the ground that he too has a flavour of himself. But I think rather we can recognise a case of what Pascal called *le style naturel*; 'when we encounter it we are quite astonished and ravished, for where we had expected to encounter an author we encounter a man.'[19] Thackeray, as Gordon Ray has indicated, is often hiding himself in his writing, rather than revealing, and so in Thackeray we encounter the author, in Trollope, the man.

Besides Tillotson and Aitkin, there has been yet another noteworthy approach to Trollope by way of style, by Hugh Sykes Davies.[20] He remarks by the way how Trollope's critics 'have been able to define his weaknesses far more clearly than his strengths.' Like Aitkin, he asserts that the plain style of Trollope is not at all a weakness but a strength; and he makes an interesting attempt to define Trollope's typical *cadence* in terms of syntax. The sentences are simple, and the characteristic structure depends on a *but* and 'the adversative *and.*' This structure functions to various ends, Davies says. It works for qualifications, or exception to a generality; it lays bare perplexities of motive in conflict, or unconscious motive; it reveals indecision; it contrasts a man's estimate of himself with our estimate; and, finally, it points the discrepancy between theory and practice. It seems to me that if grammatical analysis can tell all this about Trollope, we could do with more of it. But the ground for these perceptions are, as Davies himself says, hardly to be deduced from systematic syntactical analysis. He seems only to be making a tentative search for support of views he is already convinced of.

> For the moment, and until the input-tape punches have replaced critical hunches, it is only claimed that, *prima facie*, it looks rather as though Trollope might have a cadence after all.

Davies' well chosen examples demonstrate by example if not by logic that Trollope's writing is spare, elegant and witty: in a word, efficient.

Meantime splendid *hunches* like Davies' are the real discoveries: he assesses Trollope's 'cast of mind,' his 'quality of moral conception,' declaring him 'a passionate casuist, an observer of the relation between principles and practice,' and acclaims 'the constantly veering irony of his outlook.' This 'constantly veering irony'—as Davies' hunch has it—is the

very thing Trollope himself apprehended in his beloved
Cicero whose style is many things and none of them Trollopian.[21] Trollope more than once recognises this irony in
Cicero as the way his mind 'turned on the quick pivot on
which it was balanced.'[22] Both Cicero and Trollope are
writers who insist on the many-sidedness of things, and this
can be done either in grand baroque eloquence, or bald plain
short statements. I should say the very discontinuity of
Davies' argument is serviceable. His fine declaration of
Trollope's distinguishing qualities does *not* follow on analysis
of style, and therefore it must be the more clear to us that the
content, not the style, is of the essence.

But these analyses of Trollope's style—Aitkin's, Tillotson's,
and Davies'—have, I believe, established its qualities. And
I think it very significant that they have concertedly but
independently overthrown the old stylism that Philip Rahv
deplores. The plain, dull, flat style, the no-style style, has
been declared to be a positive artistic advantage; in refusing
to draw attention to itself it can the better display the reality
of the content. We must once more deny the old idea of
Trollope as a naïve writer. He knows what he is doing, in
style as in other matters. The agreed-on excellence of his
characterisation depends in fact on an extraordinarily subtle
sense of styles. The vulgar Major Pountney addresses Plantagenet Palliser on the subject of his country seat at Matching:

> 'A noble pile, my Lord,' said the Major, stretching his hand
> gracefully towards the building.
> 'It is a big house,'

answers Palliser (*The Prime Minister*, xxvii). One feels it
is only Trollope who could have so sharply ticked off these
two characters in confrontation.

Of course we all know form and content are not really
separable; and yet for heuristic purposes we all make the
separation. And of the two 'elements' so separated, surely
it has been form—or style—that has had a good deal of

consideration. It has been interesting and profitable to discover how writers say more than is on the surface, how they even give themselves away by their grammar and their tropes. In this kind of investigation we have the pleasure of discovering what is recondite, but we run the risk of neglecting what is patent. There is a sense in which 'content' matters enormously. To say it is the essential may be an overstatement, but it is at this stage a useful overstatement, and perhaps our best working hypothesis. In the case of Trollope, we could interest ourselves in what Aitkin calls 'the freight of moral implication,' what Tillotson calls the 'mastering of complexity,' what Davies calls the 'veering irony.' This is what Trollope meant by 'the wares he takes to market,' and what Rahv means by 'the structure of the reality portrayed.' We need to investigate the *translatable* virtues of this— comparatively—*translatable* genre, to investigate whatever it was that made Tolstoi exclaim in admiration, 'Prekrasno!' when he read Trollope's *The Prime Minister* in Russian in 1877.[23]

'Style is only one aspect of the larger concept of "form,"' and Rahv deplores not only the excesses of the critical bias of stylism, but formalism in general. Here, he has had very strong support most conspicuously in Wayne C. Booth's *Rhetoric of Fiction*.[24] Booth, more than any other single critic, has enfranchised us from the yoke of Jamesian formalism. We realise that Plot, and Point of View, and Structure, all those qualities we associate with technique, have received too much precedence. However admirable these things can be, and however brilliant their manipulation, they can all exist in work that has little value. After all considerations of technique have been exhausted, there is a residuum that is the *raison d'être* of the thing, and our *raison d'être* as critics. James deplored the English novel as *pudding*, and turned to the French, for his models and for his theory. He deplored the 'intrusive author,' and himself exploited 'point of view' with wonderful nicety as well as great artistic success. But there is more to it than James' theory allows. We begin to think that the fact that the Victorian novel is a *pudding* is its glory. Seldom has a genre been so free to be *anything*. And we find there are various values to the 'intrusion' of the author.

Albert Cook, another good instance of the new kind of thinking about fiction, is another rebel against technicism.[25] James, Flaubert, and Lubbock, he says, all 'begged the whole question of content.'[26] Cook insists on an 'inductive approach to see the meaning of fiction through the whatness of individual novels.'[27] His studies lead him to a very anti-formalist position: he suggests, at last, that the novel is the one genre which does not need 'good' structure. Indeed, 'the greater reality which the novelist discovers, the larger and more open his plots are likely to be.'[28] Anyone acquainted with Trollope will be reminded that his plots are as 'large and open' as plots can be; that he never lays any claim to 'good' structure, and critics have not claimed it for him; that, at the same time, he seems to 'discover the greatest reality.' Dickens' plots can be said to be *large*, but perhaps not *open*: he aims for some sort of drum-roll conclusion and a falling curtain at the end. And although his plots may be bad, they are nevertheless an important element in his novels. George Eliot likes to end a novel with a bang—the flood ending of *The Mill on the Floss*, for example, is troublesome because it cheats the reader somewhat, as too easy a solution to the problem set up. Even *Middlemarch*, the most Trollopian of her novels,[29] the largest and most open in plot, ends somewhat too pat, with a glimpse of the Comtean millennium. But Trollope will not sacrifice his realism to a tight plot or a pat ending. His comments on Wilkie Collins reveal his own views on this. 'The novelist has other aims than the elucidation of his plot.'[30] He admires the beautiful dovetailing of Collins' plots, but, he says, 'I can never lose the taste of the construction.'[31] He cannot do such plots himself, he says, but it is perfectly clear that he does not want to, either. In him we see the high correlation of realism with the loose plot, the correlation

Cook claims as a mark of kind of excellence in fiction. In fact, there seems to be no novelist that flouts more than Trollope those formal beauties we used to admire, and for this very reason, again, Trollope is the more liable to be useful to us as we try to discover new theory.

Rahv's essay surveys the limitations imposed by inadequate aesthetics. If we can shuffle off these, we are the more able to explore the genre. But we must be wary not only of un-useful aesthetics, but also of non-aesthetic considerations. Criticism of the Victorian novel has been much mixed up with political and philosophical elements. We discuss novels as examples of the category of propaganda novels, because it is a convenient category. And sometimes they are evaluated for their propaganda. Leavis gives the palm to *Hard Times,* because it is felt to strike at the root of the evil of the *laissez-faire* ethic. At least, such criticism does not err as formalist criticism does: it does not 'beg the question of content.' But it distorts it. Novels are documents, and can be interesting for how they affected the course of history, or recorded it, but they are not only documents. Dickens' greatness surely does not lie in his message but in his entertainment, his marvellous conjuring, the vitality of his unreality, and the supreme and glorious fact of his peculiar humour.

But just as novelists have been admitted into our Pantheon for the effectiveness of their propaganda, so also have they been admitted for what we call Serious Thought. If a Victorian novel deals with Faith and Doubt urgently enough we put it on our literature list, even if it is a deadly novel. I do not think even so great an artist as George Eliot would have got all the critical attention she has had if it had not been for her importance in intellectual history. Her art has not been neglected, but I do not think it would have got due attention if she had not first drawn us by being weightily and self-consciously philosophical. A millennial vision and Comtism can make art seem more important. Perhaps, too, it is because Hardy is self-consciously a thinker that he has been the subject of scholarship. Hardy's philosophy is not systematic, but it can be characterised, and his novels promulgate it, and so we can discuss them in terms of his philosophy. But the art remains—in Dickens, in George Eliot, in Hardy—never quite separable from the propaganda, or the philosophy, but still somewhat mysterious, and so obviously an overplus beyond the propaganda or the philosophy. Propaganda and doctrine and religious problems do not dignify Trollope's work. Perhaps in him, then, the art of the novel proper may be less dilute, and may better repay our study. Because we have not been able to talk about him in those non-aesthetic categories, and because our poetics-aesthetic has kept him out of ART, we have hardly known what to do with him. So we just read him.

But it would be good now to try to analyse his achievement, taking advantage of the present state of criticism. Some new positives emerge. We return to look at old concepts in a new light. Can mere 'characters,' after all, be vastly important? John Bayley thinks so.[32] He suggests that the author may love his people, as Chaucer does, and respect their identities, and that art gains if this is so. New religious thought posits the 'I–Thou,' and brings to mind a connection between art and morals, by means of the respect for identities. Psychologists bring attention to the concept of role-playing, and a character-oriented art may interest us the more. In what ways do men depend on roles and in what ways do they fool themselves as to their own motivations? Arthur Mizener proposes a new-old aesthetic criterion—the 'Sense of Life' in a novel: a novel is the better the more we can feel that its characters live.[33] To work out this aesthetic Mizener is not even afraid of recourse to the funny old-fashioned term *nature*, and, incidentally, one of his essays in *The Sense of Life* is an excellent study of Trollope. Out of our current interest in ethnology and anthropology we discover a new importance in men's institutions. Prometheus or Shelley or Thomas Wolfe, eating his liver

out solitarily, interest us less now, I think, than how a
particular society serves its members and they it. Perhaps we
might have already considered novels in this connection more
if we had had the terms for it. The French have: even early
in Trollope's writing career, the French critic Montégut
classified his work as *roman de moeurs*,[34] a much larger and
better label for it than our English 'novel of manners.' And
then we have a phrase now, 'aesthetic distance,' born of our
recurrent attempts to see the difference between art and mere
life. In story telling, 'aesthetic distance' appears to be involved with the nature of the narrator, and in some way the
friendship of such narrators as Chaucer, Fielding and Trollope,
appears now to be part of the art. Kathleen Tillotson exemplifies this line of thought in her important essay 'The Tale
and the Teller.'[35] In the field of fiction, these are all counts
on which the study of Trollope is à propos.

The investigation of his art is overdue. In sum, it is just
because past criticism has failed so conspicuously with him
that he may be highly useful to us in our attempts to evolve
a new criticism. Just because he least lends himself to discussion of allegory and symbol, just because his style is the
least of styles, and he appears deficient in the qualities called
formal: just because he is no propagandist, and does not
display 'Philosophy'—just because of all these things—
Trollope is now our man. Maybe he can epitomise for us anew
the Art of the Novel.

NOTES

[1]*Four Lectures*, ed. Morris L. Parrish. London, Constable, 1938.

[2]Quoted in Trollope's *Autobiography*, ed. Bradford A. Booth. Berkeley
and Los Angeles, University of California Press, 1947, p. 122.

[3]*Eight Modern Writers*. New York and London, Oxford University Press,
1963, p. 463.

[4]'My Debt to Trollope,' *The Demon of the Absolute: New Shelburne Essays*,
I. Princeton, 1928, 89–125.

[5]*Kenyon Review*, xviii, 1956, 276–299.

[6]*College English*, xvi, January, 1955, 222–225 and 232.

[7]Sherman Hawkins, 'Mr. Harding's Church Music,' *E L H* [*English Literary History*], xxix, June, 1962, 202–223.

[8]*Early Victorian Novelists*. Harmondsworth, Penguin Books, 1948, p. 199. London, Constable and Fontana, 1964.

[9]*N C F* [*Nineteenth-Century Fiction*], xx, March, 1966, 337–353.

[10]*Autobiography*, p. 197.

[11]P. 149.

[12]*Mid-Victorian Studies*. London, Athlone Press, 1965, pp. 56–61.

[13]*Autobiography*, p. 196.

[14]P. 45.

[15]'Anthony Trollope,' one of the 'Appreciations,' in *On Modern Literature*, ed. Terence Spencer and James Sutherland. New York, Oxford University Press, 1955, pp. 136–146.

[16]*Autobiography*, p. 149.

[17]'Macaulay's Style,' in *The Art of Victorian Prose*, eds. George Levine and William Madden. New York, Oxford University Press, 1968, p. 134.

[18]*Thackeray*, English Men of Letters Series. London, 1897, pp. 200–201.

[19]'Quand on voit le style naturel, on est tout étonné et ravi, car on s'attendait de voir un auteur et on trouve un homme.' *Pensées*, Edition Pléiade, p. 1096.

[20]'Trollope and His Style,' *A Review of English Literature*, i, October, 1960, 73–85.

[21]To qualify: What is usually thought of as Ciceronian style is distinctly not Trollopian; but the Cicero of the letters to Atticus—easy, intimate, witty —is a different matter. In fact, one might say Trollope's novelistic style is an extension of Cicero's epistolary style.

[22]*The Life of Cicero*, 2 vols., New York and London, 1881, i, 137; ii, 191.

[23]Quoted, N. N. Gusev, *Letopis zhizni i tvorchestra Lva N. Tolstogo*. Moscow, 1936, p. 234. I owe this item to the kindness of Professor Noel Voge. It seems that the Russians generally read their English novels in Russian translation: of Trollope's novels alone, at least thirty-one were available in nineteenth-century Russia. See Bradford A. Booth and Kenneth E. Harper, 'Russian Translations of Nineteenth-Century English Fiction,' *N C F*, viii. December, 1953, 188–197.

[24]Chicago, University of Chicago Press, 1961.

[25]*The Meaning of Fiction*. Detroit, Wayne State University Press, 1960.

[26]P. vii. [27]P. viii. [28]P. 299.

[29]T. H. S. Escott, in a very interesting passage in his *Anthony Trollope* London, John Lane, 1913, and a new edition: Bailey Bros. & Swinfen, 1968, quotes George Eliot as saying to Mrs. Lynn Linton, 'I am not at all sure that, but for Anthony Trollope, I should have ever planned my studies on so extensively a scale for *Middlemarch*, or that I should, through all its episodes, have persevered with it to the close,' p. 185.

[30]*Autobiography*, p. 194.

[31]P. 214.

[32]*The Characters of Love*. New York, Macmillan, 1960, and London, Constable, and Chatto & Windus, 1968.

[33]*The Sense of Life in the Modern Novel*, Boston, Houghton Mifflin, 1964.

[34]Emile Montégut, 'Le Roman de moeurs en Angleterre,' *Revue des Deux Mondes*, 2e période, xvii, 1858, pp. 756–788.

[35]*Mid-Victorian Studies*, London, University of London, Athlone Press, 1965, pp. 1–23.

Chapter II

THE SHAPING PRINCIPLE

'You must look to the circumstances.'

The Last Chronicle of Barset

How can we, then, talk about Trollope as an *artist*?—a man quite insouciant as to point of view, intruding himself without shame or compunction, quite as ready to tell as to show, naïvely faithful to chronological order—if he does give us a flashback it seems to be because there is something he forgot to tell—not concerned with elegance or intricacy of plot, innocent of symbol, ritual and myth. *Are* these novels anything other than random colloquies, histories, rambles? Of course they are. Mere rambles, mere history, mere photography could not conceivably hold us as these novels do. What then *can be* the controlling element, what *is* the non-random, shaping principle?

To begin at the beginning is to begin with *The Warden*, which is, as generally agreed, the start of his *oeuvre*. It has been more commented on than Trollope's other work, but I beg, nevertheless, attention for another close look at it. Or rather, let us stand back from it a little. For I believe the significance of its shape has been missed. This novel especially has suffered from our tendency to categorise: because it deals with a contemporary issue, it has been hard for us to think of it in terms other than those of the *Tendenzroman*, the novel of social purpose.

The trouble with this is that the purpose is not very clear. As propaganda, *The Warden* seems to fail. We are, in fact, puzzled to find what side Trollope is on. Is he in favour of reform or not? Apparently he does not quite know his own mind, and he suffers from a terrible indecision. A recent critic, with quick pity and ready diagnosis, finds the novel a symptom of Trollope's illness: which is the Divided Mind.[1] This is called his *plight*, and it is also the *plight* of the mid-Victorian Liberal-Conservatives. Trollope is interesting, I suppose, just because he had it worse than the others. And while so far as I know no one has found Trollope *alienated*, he nevertheless achieves chic when it is discovered that he has a 'late, dark period.'[2] So strong blow the winds of criticism.

This is the result of the persistent tradition that Trollope is a naïve writer, that *he* has no control over his material, and that his material serves to give *him* away. And then Trollope's characters seem so 'free' to develop themselves along their own lines that some critics talk as though these characters are somehow smarter than Trollope, and know more than he about motivation and morals. I think we ought to make a declaration that an author cannot be more naïve than his characters. Trollope must be at least as capable of subtle rhetoric as his dazzling lawyer Mr. Chaffanbrass, or the wily Prime Minister Mr. Daubeney; he must have at least the terrible acquaintance with the human demonic that oppresses Josiah Crawley; he must have at least the wit of Glencora Palliser, and at least her rueful understanding and love for that very trying and very admirable man her husband. Nor need we pretend to be naïve when we read Trollope's novels; as someone said of Thackeray, he really has very little appeal for the illiterate charwoman.

So, then, let us look at *The Warden* as our literate selves. We know that sinecures are by definition immoral and must be reformed. We—or Trollope's contemporaries—know, too, that the Ecclesiastical Commission is in session, and that reform is in process, and that the process will be *à l'anglaise*, that is, slow, and by degrees. Trollope is not trying to expose an abuse, nor is he trying to demonstrate the beauties of the *status quo*. His art lies in his carefulness to do neither, to avoid the *partis pris*. For it is his delight to regard the juxtaposition of the two *partis*. He has a Divided Mind, and it is no *plight*, but rather a distinct artistic advantage. *The Warden* involves both sides in a beautifully ironic demonstration of incongruities. It is a case that is richly funny in itself, and it also has a certain instructive value. Trollope exploits this case, both for its humour and for its value as enlightenment. And because of the humour, the enlightenment proceeds with as little pain to the reader as may be. Look at this case: here is a palpable abuse. The money left by Hiram's will for the benefit of twelve aged paupers has increased many fold, and it now yields chiefly a fat income for the Warden of Hiram's Hospital. But: the Warden, the instrument of this abuse, is as beneficent a man as we can imagine. Here is the *donnée*, as James would say. Here is the germ of the book. But this *donnée* is not merely the starting-point for working out an idea for a story. It *is* the book. The shape of this case is the shape of the novel.

Consider *The Warden*, by contrast, in the more usual way, as a sequential line of events. A reformer, John Bold, draws attention to an abuse: Mr. Harding, the Warden of Hiram's Hospital, is in receipt of an income far greater than intended by the original endowment. Mr. Harding gradually realises he is indeed party to an abuse, and he resigns the post. John Bold gives up the prosecution and marries Mr. Harding's daughter. Nobody wins. The only excitement at the end is not an action but a non-action: the Bishop decides to do— nothing. Surely this is a remarkably inconclusive story, and the narrative is hardly of much interest. Very early we suspect Eleanor Harding will marry John Bold, and we are not surprised when Harding resigns or when Bold gives up the case. There is not enough story-line to hold anybody.

The potency of the work is simply not in its story. It is, rather, within this situation that Trollope has taken, and in the way he exploits it. What he does, is to insist on the incongruities, by sharp juxtaposition of different perspectives. What is called his 'realism' functions to this end, and it functions like this: Not only are we told that Mr. Harding is a good man, and not only do we see him and know him as virtuous—and his virtue can only be as real as it is because he is highly individuated—not only is all this so, but further, we *love* Mr. Harding. We are involved. We know he accepted the sinecure innocently, and he performs his duties with the greatest devotion and success; he is not one to stick by the Letter of the Law—he supplies the old men with extra allowances out of his own income. He glorifies God in the excellent sweetness of his music, and the corresponding excellent sweetness of his life. But then we are involved with John Bold, too, the young idealist who devotes his labour, his medical skill, and his money to the public good, and we must love him for his principles. Readers sometimes observe that Bold is not a very sympathetic character, as though to imply that Trollope somehow fails there. But surely the limits of his charm are part of Trollope's scheme: Bold *is* in the right, and so the balance must be shifted away from him; Harding is in the wrong, and so must be made as attractive as all the novelist's virtuoso powers can make him. Nevertheless, we suffer with John Bold when Eleanor's logic of the heart has won out over his larger social logic, and he gives up his cause. He has then to face the dread Archdeacon who pounces on him with a loud 'Aha,' saying, 'You, Bold, are giving up your cause because you haven't a leg to stand on.' Bold—and we —know his cause was good. He has also to face Tom Towers of the *Times*, and be accused of knuckling under to the forces of reaction, of 'vested wrong.' In such a way do subsidiary situations develop out of the main one. It is only by casting off the demands of conventional 'plot' that Trollope is free to exploit his situation so thoroughly. He wrings his *donnée* with the sort of relentless exuberance that characterises distinguished art. By making us take cognisance of the incongruous perspectives of this case, he makes us laugh at the absurdities into which principle and precept can lead men. And he thereby catches us and leads us directly into the difficult ethical problems of the variance between seems and is, between the motive of an action and its results, between ends and means, into some understanding of the paradoxical quality of life itself.

Trollope's contemporary, Bishop Connop Thirlwall, in his important essay on the irony of Sophocles, describes the kind of situation that obliges us to reconsider our moral biases. He moves from this into his main subject, Greek tragedy and its great moral meaning. But if we stop with him at an early point in his essay, he can help us to understand the Trollopian structure. In real life, Thirlwall says,

> Our attention [will be] anxiously fixed on a struggle in which right and wrong, truth and falsehood, virtue and vice, are manifestly arrayed in deliberate opposition against each other. But still this case, if it ever occurs, is not that on which the mind dwells with the most intense anxiety. For it seems to carry its own final decision in itself. But the liveliest interest arises when by inevitable circumstances, characters, motives, and principles are brought into hostile collision, in which good and evil are so inextricably blended on each side, that we are compelled to give an equal share of our sympathy to each while we perceive that no earthly power can reconcile them. . . . What makes the contrast interesting is, that the right and truth lie on neither side exclusively: that there is no fraudulent purpose, no gross imbecility of intellect: but both have plausible claims and specious reasons to allege.[3]

Fiction uses both kinds of situations, of course. Stories that use the first kind, where 'right and wrong, truth and falsehood, virtue and vice, are manifestly arrayed in deliberate opposition,' draw our interest to the narrative itself. The interest of narrative in itself can be very great, and is, of course, perfectly legitimate. Fairy tales charm us; stories of a mystery, of a chase, of a pilgrim's progress, all can draw us from our work, our play, or our chimney corners. Or our interest may go beyond the mere narrative into some symbolic meaning or ritual usefulness that the narrative bodies forth. But the other kind of case, 'in which right and truth lie on neither side exclusively,' is compellingly interesting in itself. In art that presents this kind of case, we do not care much about narrative *per se*. In fact, the *ficta nota* works better than the mystery; Chaucer's *Troilus*, and Shakespeare's *Julius Caesar* have always been the richer for the fact that everyone knows how they are going to turn out. Narrative is not the essential, because the two sides cannot be reconciled, and there can be no real resolution. Nobody wins. This kind of art lives on realism; for the more real we feel both sides of the case to be, the more interesting and demanding the case is. Symbolic significance or ritual elements are absolutely out of place here, because they would distract from the insistent actuality of the ambivalent case which is the centre of the work, and the point of it. Sequence of events in such a work is valuable for the new and shifting perspectives it enables the author to throw on his central situation. He catches us first, perhaps by amusing us with a case in which the moral ambivalence is striking, and then he may give us pause; for we realise some theory, some precept, some generalisation is being invalidated. And there are in this, implications of very great importance. May it be that *any* theory or precept can be invalidated, in *some* case? Any case, we realise, *may* be the insistent exception, and therefore the case demands our utmost honest—and realistic—consideration. We are ethically obliged to be, then, casuists. Casuistry is a way of dealing with the practical exigencies of real life, but I should like to propose that in Trollope's work, casuistry is also a way of art. Trollope's carefully selected and significant cases constitute his content, and they also constitute the significant form of his novels.

Let us stay yet a little with *The Warden*, for it offers not only what seems to me the supremely definitive unit of Trollopian structure, but also an extra, corroborative definition of method. At this point in his career, when he has at last discovered his bent, he seems, as it were, anxious to define it for himself. I refer to the parodies of Dickens and Carlyle. Some readers find them offensive artistically, and so proceed in kindness to assess the non-offensive parts of the book, thereby missing a point. Whether these parodies succeed or not—whether they are good as parodies and whether they are decorous—they are altogether functional. Trollope is defining, by negatives, what he himself would do.

His Carlyle, Dr. Pessimist Anticant, writes a pamphlet with the heavy-handed title 'Modern Charity,' where he shows Hiram, the founder of the Hospital, as a walking angel, for he lived in the time of Abbot Samson, when all things were well; and the Warden is the typical clergyman of the present day, characterised chiefly by 'the magnitude of his appetite.' Certainly Trollope had good reason to revere the early Carlyle, and even now cannot forgo all praise; but he is chiefly anxious here to indicate Carlyle's main limitation: 'We all of us could, and many of us did, learn much from the doctor when he chose to remain vague, mysterious and cloudy; but when he became practical, the charm was gone.' Or we may say that when he got down to cases his theories did not hold. He would not recognise a certain 'fact'—'the fact, that in this world no good is unalloyed, and that there is but little evil that has not some seed in it of what is goodly' (xv). Of course, this is still the valid objection to Carlyle: he overstates his position, and then is accordingly obliged to let the end justify the means. Trollope would be a sort of watch-dog, careful to sound the alarm if precept or principle threatens to become a tyrant. He will not let ends tyrannise over means, he insists on the significance of the exception to the generality, and he would protect the minority from the majority.

The novelist, Mr. Popular Sentiment, has, like Dr. Anticant, found in the news items from Barchester a theme for a Message. In his novel, *The Almshouse,* the Warden has become a demon:

> A man well stricken in years, but still strong to do evil: he was one who looked passionately out of a hot, passionate bloodshot eye; who had a huge red nose with a carbuncle, thick lips, and a great double, flabby chin,

and so on. On the other hand, the inmates of the hospital are wonderfully good. Such is the beauty of the sentiment in their conversation that it is

> really a pity that these eight old men could not be sent through the country as moral missionaries, instead of being immured and starved in that wretched almshouse. . . . The artist who paints for the million must use glaring colours, as no one knew better than Mr. Sentiment . . . his good poor people are so very good; his hard rich people so very hard; and the genuinely honest so very honest (xv).

Both Carlyle and Dickens, Trollope would say, work by simplifications. Carlyle, to preach his sermon, has to rely on a division of phenomena into the ideal and the fallen-off from the ideal; he 'instituted himself censor of things in general,' and issued a 'monthly pamphlet on the decay of the world.' Carlyle's Sermon posits a simplistic philosophy, and Dickens' Message does the same. Accordingly, Dickens' characters are caricatures and fall into classes of Bad or Good; his ethics is caricature, too, the simplified ethics that virtue will win and vice will lose. We need not here go into the advantages and limitations of an art of simplification: all we need note here and now is that Trollope is declaring simplification is not his way. He has found in Barchester that single situation which demonstrates the complexities of moral problems, and this situation in itself is a refutation of the simplistic views of such as Carlyle and such as Dickens. Trollope is everywhere a complicator. Even in his *North America*, when he is trying to elucidate the issues of the Civil War for his English readers, he explains how the views current in England are false simplifications; he demonstrates the pros and cons on each side. His recurrent theme in the novels is that motives are never simple.

Wayne Booth, in his careful and tentative way, almost proposes that it is a special forte of the novel 'to give form to moral complexities.'[4] I think this should be proposed quite loudly. Morals *are* complex; and the only form they can take is that of the complicated, unique case. Because the novel is the loosest and potentially the longest of literary genres, the most permissive, it can take the shape of the unique case, no matter how involved or ambivalent or paradoxical, and no matter how unshapely the narrative that gives rise to it. Surely it is this forte of the novel that Trollope makes his own. This is, I think, what Geoffrey Tillotson indicates when he says Trollope 'masters complexity.'[5] The situation Trollope chooses is in itself a concrete diagram of a moral complexity; if the problem was put in abstract terms it might well escape us, but the problem of *The Warden* is—one might say—proved on our pulses. With dialogue and drama, along with clear and easy commentary (or 'intrusion'), Trollope can communicate the most tenuous nuances in a psychological state, or the most extreme subtleties in a social situation. He is like James in this, but he so 'masters complexity' that we hardly realise how complicated the things are that he has made us apprehend easily.

Trollope's interest in complex cases is thoroughly and frankly and insistently ethical. His tender casuistry demands the most careful, detailed consideration of the circumstances, even those of a 'crime,' and it is remarkable how often circumstances tend to be condoning circumstances. There are grounds in philosophy for this circumstantiality of the novel. Bertrand Russell, for instance, taking the premise that all morality must be based on immediate moral intuitions—and I suppose we must accept the premise—has this to say:

> Circumstances are apt to generate perfectly concrete convictions: this or that, now present to me, is good or bad; and from a defect of imagination, it is impossible to judge beforehand what our moral opinions of a fact will be.

A novelist like Trollope, we may say, can remedy that 'defect of imagination.' Russell continues:

> The notion that general maxims are to be found in conscience seems to me to be a mistake fostered by the Decalogue. I

should rather regard the true method of Ethics as inference from empirically ascertained facts, to be obtained in that moral laboratory which life offers to those whose eyes are open to it.[6]

Or that laboratory which, we may add, the novelist can offer. And he can offer it better than life because he can select the cases that, by invalidating general maxims, extend our understanding. The kind of novel that does this has links with various strains of nineteenth-century thought. Theorists as disparate as Emile Zola in France and George Henry Lewes in England both reprobated the separation of science and art. Science and art can both serve, it was felt, in our researches in psychology and sociology.

And there can be something like the experimental method in the novel, if it is realistic. A failure in realism is in this sense an unethical manipulation of data. Conventional plot is out of place for it may distort life processes. Once a character is established in a situation the writer must not let him act uncharacteristically for the sake of a Fourth Act crisis or a To-Be-Continued-in-the-Next-Issue cliffhanger, or a drum-roll conclusion. There must be no mysteries; we must be put in command of all relevant information as soon as possible. Trollope, of all the Victorians, is the most faithful on all these counts. He will not mystify us: time and again he tells us who did the murder or whatever. He will not let Lily Dale marry Johnny Eames, because she wouldn't have. He *says* he killed Mrs. Proudie because he overheard some clubmen saying they were sick of her. But a few sentences later he tells us the truth: 'As her tyranny increased so did the bitterness of the moments of repentance increase, in that she knew herself to be a tyrant,—till *that bitterness killed her* [my italics].'[7] It is often said in deprecation that Trollope's commonest 'plot' is the ordinary courtship plot ending in a marriage. But then, one should say in the interests of scientific accuracy, that people often do marry; and one should say in the interests of ethical research that a marriage is often the shifting of a situation in which 'the right and the truth lie on neither side exclusively'; and one might say in the interests of life that courtship and marriage are rather engaging in themselves. Trollope's last chapter marriages are generally quite probable, and though they seem like conclusions they do not necessarily make a conclusive end to a novel. It is because his endings are not generally 'conclusive,' that his characters can turn up in sequels, still breathing, aged to the proper degree, still unmistakably themselves. They had not been 'killed' by some sentimental change of heart, nor by some exigency of an elegant plot, nor by some pandering to a fictitious sensationalism. Life is sensational enough. Trollope will not suppress a murder, a suicide, a miscarriage of justice, a seduction, a bastard, a case of sexual frigidity, a case of syphilis, nor a neurosis or psychosis. Nor will he suppress a shabby motive for a 'noble' action, nor the fact that a man can be 'in love' with two women at once. Nor will he suppress the occasional emergence of what seems very like disinterested virtue.

Trollope is as realistic or as 'scientific' as conceivable, all in the interests of determining an ethics more serviceable than the simplistic ones of the abstract philosophers, and of the Sunday schools. In this he is close to George Henry Lewes, and George Eliot, but he is even closer to an older humanism. It is not enough known that he was a good Latinist, and especially devoted to Cicero. The subject of his classical learning I should like to defer to the next chapter, but for now I must mention the *De Officiis*, Cicero's closest study of ethics, and of all his works the one most revered by Trollope. The *De Officiis* reveals a strain that speaks to the Victorian, a sense of duty as strong as George Eliot's: 'Duty! How peremptory and absolute!' Cicero's mode of presentation is more urbane than hers, of course, and then so is Trollope's. In the *De Officiis*, Cicero himself is highly specific: he refers principle to particular cases, and for his particular cases he chooses those that are difficult—Thirlwallian cases or moral dilemmas—where there is much to be said on both sides.

Trollope repeatedly acclaims Cicero for this, and for his consonant rejection of systematic philosophy. He says that Cicero's great achievement is that he brings us 'out of dead intellectuality into moral perception.' And this is precisely what Trollope would do with his cases. In *The Last Chronicle of Barset*, there is a painful situation where Josiah Crawley seems to have betrayed his clerical calling by a base and petty crime. The good-hearted Robarts tries to deflect those who would impose civil law or ordinary moral maxims. 'You must look to the circumstances,' he insists. And 'You must look to the circumstances,' Trollope is always insisting, in every one of his novels. In the case of *Orley Farm*, we know that Lady Mason has committed forgery. Sir Peregrine Orme has been per *preux chevalier*, outraged that anybody might think it possible she might commit such a crime. Now he knows she has, and, heart-broken, feels he must reject her. His daughter-in-law, Mrs. Orme, pleads for her. 'In this case, though the mind of Sir Peregrine might be the more logical, the purpose of his daughter-in-law was stronger.' *She* leads Sir Peregrine 'out of dead intellectuality into moral perception'; she resolves that their friendship will withstand this evil.

> 'Do you mean,' said Sir Peregrine, 'that no crime would separate you from a friend?' 'I have not said that. *There are circumstances always* [my italics]. . . . I cannot bring myself to desert her' (XLVI).

The case, in all its peculiar individuated circumstances, must assert itself. This case, of a forger whom we cannot bring ourselves to condemn, constitutes the structure of *Orley Farm*.

Professor Gordon Ray in his illuminating and useful survey 'Trollope at Full Length'[8] has declared that Trollope's excellence is exercised most characteristically in his long novels. This is indubitably so; he needs the vast expanse of the three-decker filled with people and multiplying contingencies to demonstrate the circumstantiality of life and its ethical problems. But I think the short novels, having, of course, their own minor charms and interests, as Ray would agree, have also a special usefulness to the critic in that they display and define the Trollopian unit of structure. He was constant to his casuistic method, I believe; and I should like to turn to another short novel that is as late in his career as *The Warden* is early, and that like *The Warden* capitalises on a single ironic situation. This is the odd little novel, *The Fixed Period*, odd, because for once Trollope uses a narrator who is not himself, and because it is a piece of science-fiction, a projection into the future. It is not quite successful in the device of the narrator, and it is rather slight, but for a mere *jeu d'esprit* it has astonishing implications, and furthermore it re-exemplifies the Trollopian structural unit. This is the situation: Britannula, an island colony, has some time ago renounced British rule and is now, in about 1971, a sovereign state, under the leadership of its elected president, Mr. Neverbend (who is the narrator). The president has led the government in the adoption of a plan for euthanasia. At the age of sixty-seven (about Trollope's age when he wrote the book) all citizens are to proceed to a 'college' to undergo a speedy and painless death, or 'fixed period.' This is demonstrably a fine piece of social engineering: it perfectly solves certain pressing economic problems, and it is proved that it will benefit the state in countless ways for 'untold generations to come.' There *is* no logical objection. But of course it does not work. Trollope proceeds to amuse himself, in this little experiment, by demonstrating how rationality in mankind is not the control. He pushes accruing situations to their crises, and is able thereby to isolate and examine the irrational, and to show how the irrational, or the absurd, is of the essence, and it is just as well that it is so. He puts considerable emphasis on sport, for instance—cricket, specifically—and this is in itself to appreciate an activity that is absurd and nevertheless beneficent. In the technological progress Trollope envisages, the atom-type bomb with remote control is hardly more important than the invention of a steam cricket-pitch.

The euthanasia scheme has met with general approval, but the first case pushes every one into something like dissatisfaction. The first candidate for the college is Neverbend's close friend, who has been devoted to Neverbend and his high-minded pursuit of the greatest good of the greatest number. But he balks. Neverbend's own wife is very trying, opposing the death of their friend: 'I was going to explain to her that in a question of such enormous public interest as this of the Fixed Period, it was impossible to consider the merits of the individual cases' (IV). But he never quite gets down to explaining it, and we know this is so because it cannot be explained. Soon there is a threat of civil strife, and at last England steps in, under the direction of the Minister of Benevolence (England has progressed so far as to have such a minister, with a portfolio), and installs an English governor and takes Neverbend into custody. The Minister of Benevolence implements this step with the British Navy's atom bomb argument (so interdependent, still, are benevolence and non-benevolence). The case has asserted itself.

> 'The Parliament in England might order a three-month old baby to be slain, but could not possibly get the deed done.' 'Not if it were for the welfare of Great Britain?' 'Not to save Great Britain from destruction' (XII).

Sometimes, with Trollope, we seem to be in the company of a sort of understated Dostoevski. This *is* the problem of *Crime and Punishment*, and most specifically close to the argument with which Ivan confronts Alyosha in *The Brothers Karamazov*. Trollope's points are hardly the less telling for being made in levity. Should we not, it is asked, should we not leave death to the Almighty? Presumably we should. But then, we do not: look at wars and armies and capital punishment (X). The colony, by the way, has abolished capital punishment, but the Mother Country has not, yet.

Neverbend has by the end of the book developed into much more than a caricature; as generally in Trollope's novels, the characters seem to take their development out of the writer's hands. Finally there grows about Neverbend something of Cain, of Ethan Brand, of Svidrigailov. He himself muses on motivation: 'In considering such matters [as service to humanity], it is so hard to separate motives,—to say how much springs from some glorious longing to assist others in their struggle upwards in humanity, and how much again from personal ambition' (VII). He himself, as men go the most disinterested, has in his kindly desire for the greatest happiness of the greatest number, cut himself off from the human race—he is at last proscribed, and outlawed. His name, Neverbend, rather over-obviously indicates that we must bend to the case at hand, bend to test it in terms of the individual.

To see these short novels as demonstrating the Trollopian unit is to help us toward understanding the structure of the long, three-volume, multi-plotted panoramic books; they are, I propose, elaborations of this unit. The parts can be seen as congruent to each other and to the whole. *Barchester Towers*, for instance, expands the ironic case of *The Warden* into variations on the theme of Reform. In the ecclesiastical scene, the Proudies and Mr. Slope, although repulsive in themselves, are nevertheless the agents through whom will be purified the sons of Levi. The love passages comment on this theme of church reform: Eleanor's three suitors correspond to the three church parties, Arabin to the old High Church with all its traditions of decorum and learning; Slope to the new low evangelical party, even if he is merely riding the bandwagon of Reform for his own selfish ends; and Bertie Stanhope, the walking spirit of ecumenicism, scion of the Broad Church—*so* broad, spread so thin, that it is *no* church. In the sphere of the laity, it is the Thornes who stand for the beauty of the Old, and its absurdity, too. In religion, you recall, Miss Thorne was really a Druidess, and the Church of

England as reformed by Elizabeth I was quite modernist enough for her. The Ullathorne Games are an attempt to re-assert, however gently, the old social hierarchy, and they are, naturally, a gently ridiculous flop. Mrs. Proudie's Reception and the Ullathorne Games are both great climaxes in the structure of the novel, for in each there is the maximum juxtaposition of incongruities: Thirlwallian situations ex-foliating and contrasting with one another in algebraic progressions of absurdity. These climactic collections of situations are the centres, the *raisons d'être* of the book, much more important than how the story turns out. At the end, with Eleanor's marriage to Arabin, the focus narrows down again to Church reform, the conflict between High and Low.

> If it be essentially and absolutely necessary to choose between the two, we are inclined to agree with Mrs. Grantly that the bell, book and candle are the lesser evil of the two. *Let it however be understood* [and let me underscore this] *that no such necessity is admitted in these pages* (LIII).

The right and truth lie on neither side exclusively.

To move with Trollope from the micro-state of Barchester to the macro-state of Whitehall, is to move from the earlier novels that falter occasionally, to the later ones where he proceeds with a greater economy, a greater sophistication, and a more delicate wit. One of his finest situations is that one in *Phineas Redux* where we find the Tory Prime Minister bringing in a bill for the Disestablishment of the Church. The situation is just possible enough: it exaggerates only a *little* the audacity of Disraeli, and the ironic fact that the most radical reforms of the nineteenth century were effected under Conservative administrations. The mature Trollope exploits this situation with elegant economy and a wonderfully witty inventiveness. First: it is in a routine election speech to his constituency that Daubeney (Disraeli) makes the proposal, a speech so beautifully obscure in its rhetoric that the electors of East Barsetshire have no idea what he is saying. They take 'more actual enjoyment from the music of his periods than from the strength of his argument.' They enjoy the references to clerical matters; the word *mitre* 'sounds pleasantly in their ears as appertaining to good old gracious times' (v). It is only as a double-take that the newspapers and public discover Disestablishment has been proposed. And then we have grand general consternation everywhere. London swarms with the buzz of activated and anxious clergymen. The Tory party is in an agony of strained loyalties: shall the Tory member vote to support the party he loves, and thereby support this flashy 'Cagliostro' whom he inclines to distrust even though he keeps the party in power? And shall he thereby vote against the Establishment he stands for? And then there is the suffering Opposition, absolutely dished by this cruel move which takes Reform out of the hands of those whose proprietary interest it is. Shall the Liberal member vote against this bill, in loyalty to his party and in the hopes of turning out the Tory administration so that *his* party will then be in power and proceed with Reform? And shall he thereby vote against a measure which takes a grand step toward the ideal society he strives for? The wily Daubeney asks: is it not best that reform of the church be by our means who best revere her? And, of course, he can accuse the Opposition of a great lack of principle and an unseemly lust for power. Trollope delays the narrative and explores the repercussions of this pregnant situation, thereby exploring the nature of man as political animal. He discovers in actualities those truths Walter Bagehot discovers in theory in *The English Constitution*: that there must, for instance, be a degree of party loyalty or parliament simply cannot achieve anything; and whenever there is a degree of party loyalty there is a degree of personal integrity sacrificed. This is the abiding great problem of the relation of truth to politics that Hannah Arendt has recently reappraised.[9] Trollope's service is that he demonstrates the relationship so dynamically, in terms of such a variety of irresistibly interesting people, that we cannot help but grow in political understanding.

The two *Phineas Finn* novels are that part of Trollope's work which might be classified structurally as a loose sort of *Bildungsroman*. And yet I think that they too, like the other novels, are best considered as situation-structured. So considered, they are really not very loose. For this grand situation of the Tory bill for Disestablishment is the extension of Phineas' own problem of adjusting his honesty to political usefulness. One minor but related situation, for example, finds Phineas standing for a rotten borough so that he can get into Parliament so that he can effect the abolition of rotten boroughs. And then, in his complicated love-life, we see him so obstinately and contrarily honest as to demand from one discarded sweetheart the warm sympathy and help he wants to win the new one. All these related anomalous situations comment on one another and together constitute a cogent form for the novel.

Jerome Thale has addressed himself to 'The Problem of Structure in Trollope' by means of a perceptive examination of *The Last Chronicle of Barset*.[10] Trollope has been so often reprehended, Thale observes, for being loose and rambling that we wonder 'whether we ought to hedge about his greatness.' Thale proceeds to show that indeed we ought not to hedge, and he demonstrates that the construction of this novel depends upon 'not the succession of events, but the accumulation of them, and the grouping of events and characters.' The method itself, he says, produces a new perspective, and is 'the means through which Trollope's wonderful disenchanted clarity of vision, his tolerance and accuracy, operate to produce a remarkably complex and balanced vision of human life.' Trollope's novels have the effect of 'reminding us of the complexity of human affairs, or urging tolerance, of making us wary of simple views and monisms.' This seems to me to have the ring of nothing less than the truth; Thale does indeed demonstrate the unity, and assesses the effect. However, as he himself says, mere thematic unity can hardly explain such an effect. But I think when the unity is seen as controlled by *case*-structure, then the congruency of form and function becomes apparent.

The ethical ends of Trollope's art appear to be best served by his situation-structure. His concern is always moral, and he is always recommending, by means of his cases, a more flexible morality. His stance is that of what we now call Situation Ethics, and I propose that he has a corresponding Situation Aesthetics. His ethics and his aesthetics, that is, are functions of each other, both turning on casuistry. The art of it makes us see the uniqueness of character in circumstances, and the end of it is moral perception. It is a very satisfactory thing that the means to this end is so delightful that we can take the means for end, and the end still achieves itself.

One of the incidental pleasures of the novels is Trollope's positively virtuoso display of a variety of lawyers in action. His interest in lawyers and the law, however, is not really incidental, but a significant aspect of his Situation Ethics. The lawyer is on principle dedicated to the uniqueness of cases. Trollope shares with Cicero a sense of the law as the imperfect but best human effort to implement the excellent idea of Justice, which Cicero saw as though innate and as the omen that man is, after all, worth troubling with. There is in both Cicero and Trollope a consequent ultimate optimism about human destiny, in spite of all appearances. Appearances were bad enough in Cicero's time, as Trollope points out, when everything of the old republican tradition and everything of political honesty was doomed. For Trollope, the vision of society in *The Way We Live Now* is bad enough: he sees how prevalent is our willingness to come to terms with evil, if there is something in it for us. And yet it is his idea that even the worst of us has a right to an advocate, and his legal cases are only more technically casuistic than his other cases. In *Orley Farm*, Lady Mason commits forgery out of love for her son. In her worst agonies of guilt, she pleads (or Trollope does) that she has put her son ahead of the safety of her soul. Trollope displays at least twenty perspectives on the relation of law to justice in this case, each one viable because each one is in terms of the view of an actualised character. The late novel *Mr. Scarborough's Family* is a marvellously manoeuvred case where law and justice run quite at odds. And yet Mr. Scarborough who so deliberately and cleverly perverts the law to his own ends is not all bad, is admirable in his *virtù*, and is motivated by a kind of extra-legal sense of justice. We follow the touching disillusionment of lawyer Grey, who had dedicated himself to the law in the faith that it does indeed march with justice. In *Phineas Redux*, there is what Harold Laski called the best murder trial in modern literature. Phineas, whom we know to be not only innocent but a man who is the least liable to commit a crime, is accused of a vengeful and brutal murder. The great criminal lawyer, Chaffanbrass, manipulates the Court, and ourselves, with such eloquence that we cannot believe anyone there present could any longer have any doubt whatsoever as to Phineas' innocence; and then we see Chaffanbrass retired to a little room, exhausted and old in the service of the law, brooding on what he thinks to be the 'fact' of Phineas' guilt. So curious are the processes of this man-made institution the law; such may be the wisdom in the odd principle that the lawyer's belief in his client's innocence is irrelevant to his duty as advocate. We see justice done: Phineas is released and exonerated. But we see him far from joyful. The bitterness of his ordeal has left him in a depression, incapacitated for a while at least. Justice at best is not enough to alleviate the soreness of man's cruelty to man.

Trollope and the law is a subject that has been studied closely and lovingly by those distinguished lawyers who have been Trollopians. For us, the point of it might be put this way: It is Trollope's art to be advocate for each one of his characters; he makes the best case possible for one, and then juxtaposes this with the demands of the other, defended with a similar passionate sympathy. His art is distinguished by largeness of view, encompassing the conflicting claims of all his people and of society. His great achievement, often just called being 'good at characterisation,' may be really that he communicates his characters' sense of self. It is his own lively sense of the uniqueness of personality that not only makes him a great artist of character but also leads him to his Situation Ethics. And this is really another name for the old humanistic idea of man as the measure of things. So it is that Trollope presents life always in terms of human beings all with claims nearly as valid as one's own. His art is responsible to society; his novels, being organised according to specific challenging cases, do in fact implement a casuistic ethics. The old idea of Trollope as a purveyor of escape will hardly do; if there is a logical opposite to *escape*, that is what Trollope's novels are. He takes us into the centre of life, obliging us to recognise incongruities, forcing the appreciation of the dilemma. The novels are, in a way, more demanding than life itself generally is, and in reading them one as it were flexes one's moral entity and exercises one's humanity.

NOTES

[1]John H. Hagan, 'The Divided Mind of Anthony Trollope,' *NCF*, xiii, June, 1959, 1–26.

[2]A. O. J. Cockshut, *Anthony Trollope: A Critical Study*. London, Wm. Collins Sons & Co. Ltd., 1955, and New York, New York University Press, 1968.

[3]'On the Irony of Sophocles,' *The Philological Museum*, ii, 1833, 483–537.

[4]*The Rhetoric of Fiction*. Chicago, 1961, p. 188.

[5]'Trollope's Style,' *Mid-Victorian Studies*, pp. 56–61.

[6]*Autobiography*. Boston, Little, Brown, 1967, p. 253.

[7]*Autobiography*. London, Allen & Unwin, 1967, 1968, pp. 230–231.

[8]*Huntingdon Library Quarterly*, xxxi, August, 1968, 313–340.

[9]'Reflections: Truth and Politics,' *New Yorker*, February 25, 1967, pp. 49–88.

[10]*NCF*, xiv, September, 1960, 147–157.

Chapter III

CLASSICAL CASES

Quid est quo praescriptum aliquod aut formulam
exprimas, cum in suo quodque genere praestat et genera
plura sint?

Cicero, *Orator*

PERHAPS this situation-structure of the novels, once
recognised, implies in itself a degree of intellectual sophistication not traditionally part of the old naïve Trollope, the
'artless' chronicler of the ordinary. Is there in fact a philosophical fulcrum for this wide-ranging deployment of ambivalent situations? One ought to be able to determine Trollope's
rationale, if he has one: traditionally the most 'artless' he
nevertheless wrote more theory than any other Victorian
novelist.[1] A good part of the *Autobiography* is literary criticism,
and we have his study of Thackeray, a great number of
magazine and occasional pieces, as well as his letters. The
most significant instances of his theorising may be those many
discursions in the novels themselves, written from the very
centre of operations. But we need caution in excising them,
for they are tightly tied to their contexts. As with Fielding
and Sterne, these occasional discourses on the art are themselves part of the art. They serve to affirm the frank relationship between author and reader, to affirm their common
ground as ironic observers, and to effect what is called
'aesthetic distancing.'

His overt criticism might be expected to give us more
help, but here we must be still cautious, for, as I see it, two
main reasons. The first is simply that Trollope is a better
artist than theorist; he wrote better than he knew. He had
not the advantage of much precedent theory of fiction, the
English novel being, as James said, not yet *discutable*. It is no

wonder that he did not achieve an aesthetic of fiction when we are even now still floundering. But rather it is something of a wonder that he was so often impelled to hew out elements of a theory, so original as to conceive of a history of English fiction, and often so very searching in the insights he did record. He certainly never fell into dogmatism. 'I am not sure,' he wrote after years of successful practice, 'that I have as yet got the rules quite settled in my mind.'[2] It is hard not to be distracted by the modest grace of this remark; but it must be noted anyway how it demonstrates his pervading empiricism. He will speak with confident judgment on an author or a book, but he will guard himself on the generality.

A second reason for caution in interpreting his statements on the art lies in his own nature, his ironic under-statement. When the American woman asked him how he chose the *words* for his novels, he answered that of course he chose the longest because they fill up the pages quickest.[3] He is often teasing, too, when he flaunts the methodicalness of his work, or compares it to that of the shoemaker. There is a serious undertone, however: his social or commercial conscience obliges him to deliver the best he can for his hire, to his publishers and to his readers. He does not consider the responsibility an inconvenience to the artist; it is altogether proper, and may be the spur to more kinds of art, even, than 'mere' novels. He makes a significant passing reference to Shakespeare, who in 'sitting down to write *a play that might serve his theatre* [italics mine] composed some *Lear* or *Tempest* —that has lived and will live forever, because of the genius that was unknown to himself.'[4] He keeps running a gentle mockery of romantic theories of inspiration. Our Trollope is no Aeolian harp waiting for a divine wind to blow through *him*. He sees the artist in the centre of the busy-ness of human life, subject to its strictures and responsibilities. And when he defends 'English Prose Fiction as a Rational Amusement'[5] even his title is deflationary. He suggests that novelists who expect to reform institutions or to help effect a grand

Comtean millennium may be somewhat overweening. He opposes to the reformer's zeal his own classical sense of the continuity of man's experience and his acceptance of the state of things in general, that George Eliot rather significantly remarked on: he is 'a Church of England man, clinging to whatever is, on the whole.'[6] Such a man as Horace, Trollope writes in a particularly interesting letter, 'Horace, who is playful and even good-natured in his very satyres [sic], did probably teach men to be less absurd.'[7] *There* is a modest statement for the aim of art, *there* is Rational Amusement. And *there*, in Trollope's classical sense of moderation, in his humanistic stance, is to be found, I believe, the clue to his quality.

There is an item among his non-fiction in which I think he defines himself with particular clarity. I mean his two-volume study of Cicero. He wrote it between 1877 and 1880, probably the period of his ripest thought and greatest artistic power. It belongs to the same period as his *Autobiography*, and it is hardly to be preferred to the *Autobiography* in general interest. But where the *Autobiography* is informal, intimate and off-the-cuff, the *Cicero* is carefully considered and deliberate. Where the *Autobiography* was written to be published after his death, the *Cicero* is a piece of scholarship that Trollope was ready to be answerable for. It is certainly his longest literary study, and he makes it, I believe, the occasion of his most considered and direct statements on life and art and morals. The novels themselves are certainly the richest statement of his views, but here, in the *Cicero*, one may find the literal and discursive formulation of the attitudes that make the novels what they are.

The whole subject of Trollope's Latin studies is important both for his biography and his art. I think Frank Pierce Jones is right when he intimates that Latin had a symbolic value for Trollope.[8] In his youth of humiliating poverty, his failure at Latin was a token of his general failure, token of the ill-fitting clothes, of the sense of being outcast, of the foregoing of what he might have called his birthright as a gentleman. The classics were still the distinguishing education of a gentleman, although exposure rather than proficiency often seemed to be the principle. But for Trollope, Jones suggests that the turning point against failure, in his days as Post Office clerk, was his mastering on his own the Latin he had failed in at Harrow and Winchester; it may well have been this that first gave him the confidence which circumstances had denied him. His favourites are Cicero and Horace. I think he early sensed in them the urbanity and the ironic temper that he yearned for. He did achieve an easy mastery of Latin and took a moral satisfaction in that; and he found further satisfaction in these two writers so deeply sympathetic to his own spirit. To live in their company was to foster his own ironic temper of mind and to share in their humane grace.

The book on Cicero is a labour of love to him. He finds current a misreading of his character, and loving the man, loves to defend him. It is Caesar the opportunist who gets the praise rather than Cicero, praise very little qualified, from the historians Macaulay, Merivale, Mommsen, Froude.[9] Trollope takes exception to the idealisation of Caesar (and perhaps also thereby to the Carlylean Hero): 'The one [Caesar] has been lauded because he was unscrupulous, and the other [Cicero] has incurred reproach because, at every turn in his life, scruples dominated him.'[10] Men—even learned historians—actually admire success, although they may think they admire moral excellence. So Trollope sees the struggle between Caesar and Cicero as rich in a moral meaning that is as relevant now as when the course of the Western world depended on the outcome. True, Trollope grants, Caesar was never cruel for the sake of cruelty; but this is not enough. For Caesar was never deterred by 'humanity' from what was expedient.[11] 'To say that Caesar was justified in the armed position which he took in Northern Italy [in 50 B.C.] is to rob him of his praise.' The method of the man was to defy law and justice. If you admire Caesar, you must admire him as lawbreaker. But 'there are some of us who think that such a man, let him be ever so great . . . will in the end do more harm than good.'[12] The criterion lies in pity. 'They who can see a Cicero struggling to avoid the evil that was coming—not for himself but for the world around him—and can lend their tongue, their pens, their ready wits to ridicule his efforts, can hardly have been touched by the supremacy of human suffering.'[13] Trollope insists that where 'humanity' never affected Caesar's line of action, it was Cicero's constant point of reference.

Cicero has been accused of being a turncoat, in that terrible period when the balance of power shifted with such violent rapidity. But Trollope makes the case for him that he acted with unswerving devotion to the public good (and this represents a position still respectable among classical scholars). To keep humanity—pity—as the touchstone is to renounce consistency and bend to the occasion.[14] Hence it is that Cicero's own case demonstrates the complexities of morals, and the necessity for relativism—he often had to take the lesser of two evils. How difficult, for instance, the exercise of mere honesty is, for the good man in public life. 'At one moment,' writes Trollope in his *Cicero*,

> the rule of simple honesty will prevail with him. *Fiat justitia, ruat caelum.* . . . At another he will see the necessity of a compromise for the good of the many. He will tell himself that if the best cannot be done, he must content himself with the next best. He must shake hands with the imperfect, as the best way of lifting himself up from a bad way towards a better.

And now he states the irony in its extreme form:

> In obedience to his very conscience he will temporise, and finding no other way of achieving good, will do even evil that good may come of it. *Rem si possis recte; si non, quocunque modo rem.*[15]

We see these problems dramatised in the careers of Trollope's Plantagenet Palliser and Phineas Finn.

Trollope finds Cicero himself deeply aware of the ironic nature of the dilemma. In quoting Cicero, he returns again and again to statements like this: 'a captain in making a port cannot always sail thither in a straight line, but must tack and haul and use a slant of wind as he can get it.'[16] (This particular one is echoed in *The Last Chronicle*, LXII.) Or, 'the very possession of power is an evil in itself. But without that evil you cannot have the good which the institution contains.'[17] And because of Cicero's own awareness of moral implications, his decisions as a politician—as *homme engagé*—are worthy of our study. Trollope speaks of Cicero's dilemma, for instance, when it was open to him to conspire with Caesar against Pompey.

> The bait was held out to him, as it is daily to others, in a form not repellent, with words fitted to deceive and powerful almost to persuade. Give us the advantage of your character, and then by your means we shall be able to save our country. Though our line of action may not be strictly constitutional, if you will look into it you will see it is expedient. What other course is there? How else shall any wreck of the Republic be preserved? Would you be another Cato, useless and impractical? Join us, and save Rome to some purpose. We can understand that in such a way the lure was held out to Cicero, as it has been to many a politician since. But when the politician takes the office offered to him—and the pay, though it be but that of a Lord of the Treasury—he must vote with his party.[18]

Problems like this, not only in politics, are rich stuff for the novelist, rich in the ironies of *seems* and *is*, of pretension and actuality, of rationality and absurdity, of principle and practice.

The intimate record of the letters to Atticus afford an insight into this perhaps unparalleled example of a brilliant mind forever politically engaged. Trollope sees him as 'a vane turning on a pivot finer than those on which statesmen have generally been made to work.'[19] His own honesty shines the brighter for the corruption of the age.[20] He was 'no Cincinnatus, no Decius, no Camillus, no Scipio . . . no demigod . . . but one who at every turn was conscious of his human duty, and anxious to do it to the best of his human ability.'[21] There is heroism even in his refusal to accept the imminent doom of the old Republic.[22] Parallels with Bacon occur to Trollope, that further enhance Cicero's heroism:

> They were both great lawyers, both statesmen, both men affecting the *omne scibile*, and coming nearer to it than perhaps any other whom we can name; both patriots, true to their conceived idea of government, each having risen from obscure position to great power, to wealth, and to rank; each from his own education and his nature prone to compromise, intimate with human nature, not over-scrupulous either as to others or as to himself. They were men intellectually above those around them, to a height of which neither of them was himself aware. To flattery, to admiration, to friendship, and to love each of them was peculiarly susceptible. But one failed to see that it behooved him, because of his greatness, to abstain from taking what smaller men were grasping; while the other swore to himself from his very outset that he would abstain—and kept the oath which he had sworn.[23]

Trollope divides his study of Cicero into two parts, the first a Life, the second a methodical consideration of the Works, showing how the moral orientation of the life informs the man's writings. Cicero knew complexity and rejected the simplistic; and the artistic correlative of this position is that complex of things we call *irony*, which itself depends on the ability to appreciate incongruities and to correlate them. Hence it is that Kenneth Burke has well defined it as 'the perspective of perspectives.'[24] The word *irony* Trollope uses only in its narrower sense of stylistic or verbal irony, and of course he acclaims this stylistic irony:

> With Cicero we are charmed by the modernness, by the tone of today which his language takes. The rapid way in which he runs from scorn to pity, from pity to anger, from anger to public zeal, and then instantly to irony and ridicule, implies a lightness of touch, which not unreasonably surprises us as having endured for so many hundred years.[25]

But he appreciates the larger aspects of Cicero's irony, the achievement of the 'perspective of perspectives,' perhaps most clearly when he speaks of the way his thoughts would turn round on that 'quick pivot on which they were balanced.'[26] He loves the largeness of mind, and he loves the wit that comes from the ability to see the many sides of an issue and from the artistic control that such a view affords. Trollope observes there was no moment of Cicero's life when he was not able to laugh.[27]

Such a man is good company. Trollope quotes Martial: if the traveller 'have but a book of Cicero's writing he may fancy he is travelling with Cicero himself.'[28] Cicero is a supreme letter writer, but it is not only in the letters that we have the sense of his companionship. Perhaps it happens that the ironic writer, in exploiting his position as friend to the reader, is extending the genre of epistle into the essay or novel. I think this is so of Montaigne, and of Charles Lamb. And I think it is so to a great extent also of Fielding, of Sterne, and of Trollope.[29] At any rate, we note Trollope's appreciation of this friendship with the author who was a specialist on *Amicitia*.

What a man he would have been for London life! How he would have enjoyed his club, picking up the news of the day from all lips, while he seemed to give it to all ears! How popular he would have been at the Carlton, and how men would have listened to him while every great or little crisis was discussed! How supreme he would have sat on the Treasury bench, or how unanswerable, how fatal, how joyous, when attacking the Government from the opposite seats! How crowded would have been his rack with invitations to dinner! How delighted would have been the middle-aged countesses of the time to hold with him mild intellectual flirtations—and the girls of the period, how proud to get his autograph, how much prouder to have touched the lips of the great orator with theirs! How the pages of the magazines would have run over with little essays from his pen! 'Have you seen our Cicero's paper on agriculture? That lucky fellow,

Editor ——, got him to do it last month!' 'Of course you have
read Cicero's article on the soul. The bishops don't know
which way to turn.' 'So the political article in the *Quarterly*
is Cicero's?' 'Of course you know the art-criticism in the
Times this year is Tully's doing?' But that would probably be
a bounce.[30] And then what letters he would write! With the
penny-post instead of travelling messengers at his command,
and pen instead of wax and sticks, or perhaps with an instru-
ment-writer and a private secretary, he would have answered
all questions and solved all difficulties. He would have so
abounded with intellectual fertility that men would not have
known whether most to admire his powers of expression or to
deprecate his want of reticence.[31]

The pleasure of Cicero's friendship lies not only in his charm
and brilliance but in his goodness also. Like Erasmus, Trollope
loves Cicero 'not only for the divine felicity of his style, but
for the sanctity of his heart and morals.'[32] Somehow, if one
cannot count on an author's probity, what he says is invalidated. In this respect it is good to recall the pervading importance in Trollope's novels of the concept of the 'gentleman,'
and how the concept is practically an extension of Christian
morals into manners, a sort of 'sanctity of heart and morals.'
Manners are no superficial concern, often constituting as they
do the 'case' where morals are to be applied. It is Edith
Hamilton's opinion that 'the gentleman, the English gentleman, who has meant much to many generations, may well
have had his beginnings in, certainly he was fostered by, the
English schoolboy's strenuous drilling in Cicero.'[33]

Trollope found in Cicero a tenderness for humankind that
is like his own. It is the root—in both Cicero and Trollope—
of zest for life and of a persistent optimism. At times things
went so badly for Cicero, Trollope writes, that 'the reader,
knowing the manner of Romans, almost wonders that he
condescended to live!'[34] Elsewhere in the book Trollope
discusses how Cicero was both in principle and practice
opposed to suicide, and then at various points in the novels he
himself takes up this question of all questions. But the central

fact is that Cicero, and Trollope too, did knowingly condescend to live because both sensed something to revere in mankind. Both knew the irony of the good within the evil. There is, says Cicero, 'that God within us [that] forbids us to depart hence without his permission.'[35] This good within the evil demands our service, for 'all duty'—this is Trollope translating Cicero again—'which tends to protect the society of man with men is to be preferred to that of which science is the simple object.'[36] Like Trollope, Cicero has a way of extending an idea into individual cases: he declares it is man's duty to 'study the welfare of all over whom he stands in the position of master,' even slaves, even beasts![37] This kind of *humanitas* is what supports the novelist in extending understanding and sympathy over a broad range of characters.

Much of Cicero's career was in law, and this gives Trollope the occasion to discuss the ethics of advocacy which is so closely related to his novels. And the great question here is, can the lawyer in good conscience undertake the defence of the man he knows to be guilty? Or can he as a just man take sides at all? Trollope has much to say on Cicero's legal ethics; to take only one example, he says that Cicero himself

> explains very clearly his own ideas as to his own speeches as an advocate, and may be accepted, perhaps, as explaining the ideas of barristers of today. 'He errs [Cicero says] who thinks that he gets my own opinions in speeches made in law courts; such speeches are what the special cases require, and are not to be taken as coming from an advocate as his own.'[38]

There is no question of the delight in debate as virtuosity or the joy of the battle, and Trollope and his readers find this vicarious delight in the legal parts of the novels. But Trollope has a sense of the high purpose the advocate serves and quotes Cicero: 'The greatest praise comes from defending a man accused; and especially so when you shall assist one who is surrounded and ill-treated by the power of some great man.'[39]

The matter of advocacy implies more than all this, however;

it is, as I have suggested above, related to artistic method. It would seem, indeed, that the advocate must deliberately forego the double ironic perspective. But I would say it is ultimately only by means of advocacy that the detached ironic judgment can be achieved. The judge must know each case as an individual case in its most extreme statement, before the juxtaposition of case with case has value. So the advocate performs his service in presenting his client in the best possible light; it is his function to give him all conceivable benefits of the doubt. Our duty to that 'God within' even the worst of men demands advocacy. That duty leads Trollope even to find the grain of good in what started as a caricature; he extorts our sympathy at last even for Mrs. Proudie. He can see even into the murky consciousness of the scoundrel Melmotte. The law and the machinery of advocacy are bound up with Trollope's art, just as they are bound up with Cicero's.

But of all Trollope's study of Cicero, perhaps the most revealing for us is that part where he takes up Cicero's philosophy, for it shows, I believe, Trollope's own intellectual attitude. The attitude is not paraded in the novels, and may be a little difficult to discover, especially if one looks for a system. And it would seem that literary critics do look for a system. Some of the comments on Trollope as non-thinker seem to imply that we can expect a systematic philosophy from any artist worth his salt. Professional philosophers do not, so far as I can see, expect so much from philosophy. I think it can be shown that Trollope's own position consists in 'antisystematism,' and that it is a deliberate, considered position, and that it is in itself basic to an extraordinarily humane artistic product. What then is Cicero's actual position? It is a moot point whether we can call it philosophy; as the word philosophy shifts in usage, so have the assessments of Cicero as philosopher. We can nevertheless categorise to some extent. There are two questions that have been at times confused: one, what are his services to the discipline of philosophy? and two, what is his own original thought? His services to philosophy are inestimable. His aim was to make available in Latin the best thought of those prolific thinkers, the Greeks. What he gives us are summaries, with his own comments, of all the Greek schools; and, for the most part, we do not have his originals to check him against. Fortuitously, he himself is our source for much late Greek philosophy. It is an interesting irony that Cicero's style preserved for posterity the thought of philosophers who generally on principle repudiated literary values. Then, because Cicero has given us the greater part of our philosophical terms, as he translated or imported Greek words into Latin, he has controlled our thinking immeasurably. He himself was a man much aware of the interdependence between *res* and *verba*, and his *verba* have, willy-nilly, shaped our *res*. One may attack any proposition of Cicero's, but it is likely that one will have to do it in Cicero's terms.

To determine his own philosophy proper, in the old sense, is not easy. The list of his works that involve philosophy is long, and most of them are in the form of dialogue, with much dramatic play between speakers. He generally allows each school the best possible rationale, through the voices of his charming and persuasive friends. Cicero's legal art made him adept at putting the *case* for any view, and likewise adept at finding the loopholes in any case. Herein lie the interest and delight of these philosophical discourses, and herein also lies the difficulty of determining his own thought. He has been all things to all men; in his works one can find a statement to support almost anything. And yet this is a clue to his quality. The only school he can safely be assigned to is the New Academy. The principle of the New Academy, as of Socrates, is to argue against every proposition and to pronounce positively on nothing. The only certainty is that the wise man suspends judgment; he nurtures the sceptical mind. It is true that the New Academy might, then, be better characterised as a perennial attitude rather than a 'school.' Yet even today the attitude constitutes something of a school: the school of those linguistic philosophers who oppose themselves to the formalism of logical positivism. Their activity often actually seems to consist in begging questions. And hence it is that 'philosophy,' now as for Socrates, can denote not so much a content but a method.

Cicero can best be thought of as the proponent of a method, and in this he is antisystematic, antitheoretical and anti-dogmatic. He makes fun of the Stoics, for instance, for even among themselves they agree on very little; and, as he points out with stunning logic, the contradictory factions within the Stoic fold cannot all be right, and only one can possibly be right. He adds, moreover, that probably none is right. It would seem that no theory whatsoever is unassailable, and therefore Cicero reprobates theory as such. In all this, Cicero typifies the Roman way, only that he is perhaps the most articulate Roman of them all. He speaks for the practical Roman rather than for the idealist Greek, more realistic than theoretical, more human than philosophical. His most knowledgeable critics are agreed that his original contribution to philosophy is really a division of the field into two, the first, speculation on abstract problems, and the second, the consideration of human affairs. In the one, abstract speculation, scepticism is proper; but in the other, all matters of ethics, morals or duty, there must be dogmatism. Philosophical speculation may be a delightful exercise, but the study of ethics is man's pressing need. And, when Cicero expounds duty, there is no equivocation.

It is this position of Cicero's that Trollope so perfectly apprehends when he insists that Cicero takes us 'Out of dead intellectuality—into moral perception.'[40] That he was impeccably learned, Trollope has no doubt. 'He had been in the schools at Athens, and had learned it all.'[41] He tells us the circumstances of Cicero's philosophical writing, his terrible year, near the end of his life, when he was cut off from politics and even from his books, as well as heart-broken over the death of his daughter; it is supposed that it was to console himself that he wrote philosophy. Trollope comments:

> As we read these works, we lose ourselves in admiration of his memory; we are astonished at the industry which he exhibits; we are delighted by his perspicuity; and feel ourselves relieved amid the crowd of names and theories by flashes of his wit; but there comes home to us, as a result, the singular fact of a man playing with these theories as the most interesting sport the world had produced, but not believing the least in any of them.[42]

The theories are simply irrelevant.

> Out of all the sixty-four years of his life he devoted one to this philosophy . . . and so lived during all these years, even including that one, as to show how little hold philosophy had upon his conduct. . . .[43] I have great doubt whether consolation in sorrow is to be found in philosophy, but I have none as to the finding of it in writing philosophy.[44]

The consolation, of course, lies in the work.

When Trollope makes the point that Cicero was committed to no school, he makes a particularly revealing comment: 'He was too honest, too wise, too civilised, too modern for that.'[45] When he says Cicero was too honest to adhere to any system, is he not saying that for himself it would be dishonest to adhere to any system? When he says Cicero was too wise to adhere to any system, is he not saying that his own intellect rejects it? Then, when he says Cicero was 'too civilised, too modern' to adhere to any systematic philosophy, surely it is clear that Trollope himself considers it both naïve and outworn. Trollope is always too modest or too given to understatement to proclaim an intellectual superiority, but I think it is nevertheless true that he felt himself above and beyond 'philosophy.' 'Out of dead intellectuality—into moral perception'—and this is precisely where Trollope would take us in the novels. Those critics who complain of Trollope's lack of 'philosophy' are demanding what Trollope would have called 'dead intellectuality.' His novels do, in fact, deflate intellectuality, by the presentation of actual cases which negate commonly accepted theories, or systems or precepts. Trollope demonstrates that absolutes can fail us in the affairs of life and can even betray us into uncharity.

The book where Cicero makes ethics most specifically his business is the one Trollope admires beyond all others. It is the *De Officiis*, the treatise Cicero writes *in propria persona* to his son *propriae personae*, and in it Cicero addresses himself not to those easy cases like murder or theft where all men agree on the evil, but to the difficult ones, the moral dilemmas, where the course of virtue is obscure. The importance of the *De Officiis* in Trollope's work is inestimable. When he explicates *honestum*, the central concept of the treatise, he gives in effect that definition of the concept of the 'gentleman' that he impatiently refuses us in the *Autobiography*. The concept is central to the whole of the moral vision of his work. Even the structure of the *De Officiis* supplies the structure for many of the situations in the novels. Cicero contrasts *honestum* with *turpe*, and Trollope is often concerned to determine whether the right course demands positive action, or whether mere inaction is sufficiently better than wrong-doing. His *Cousin Henry* is the most precise example of a study of this *turpe* as opposed to *honestum*.[46] In this short novel everything is focused on the single significant case. Henry takes no evil action; but, by failing to take the virtuous action, he becomes despicable. The problem extends itself in the long 'panoramic' novel *The Way We Live Now* where *turpe* takes many forms in many cases, and Trollope is concerned to show how great evil springs from mere acquiescence in slight evils.

A second large subhead in the *De Officiis* is the relating of *honestum* to *utile*; and this relationship is a recurrent and endlessly interesting theme in Trollope, as he takes up those many cases where principle and expediency seem to be at odds, in sexual selection, in law, in problems of Church and government. Moral perception, it seems, is to be achieved only through the most meticulous examination of the individual

case, all sides of it, its history, the motivation of each agent
involved, the results of action or inaction, repercussions in
many directions. 'You must look to the circumstances.' This is
really why Trollope's work is so 'circumstantial,' so involved
with minutiae of psychology and manners. For these minutiae
can concertedly twist moral perspectives in unpredictable ways.
Virtue is seldom a matter of black and white, as popular
morality holds it to be, and like Cicero in the *De Officiis*
Trollope chooses those cases where it is least a matter of black
and white; hence, moral dilemmas, the most difficult cases of
all, where principle is demonstrably inadequate and our
understanding of things must be extended. To determine
virtue is the only concern really worthy of our study, and it is,
in a way, the only interesting study.

If morals are always a relative matter, where then can we
find any certainty? The certainty has to be an empirical one.
And Trollope found in Cicero a satisfactory statement of this
sole certainty. It was not to be found in any formal 'philosophy,' Trollope insists, but he speaks of Cicero's 'true
philosophy,' that was 'the real guide of his life.'

'Among things which are honest,' he [Cicero] says, 'there is
nothing which shines so brightly and so widely as that brotherhood between man, that agreement as to what may be useful
to all, and that general love for the human race. It comes
from our original condition, in which children are loved by
their parents; and then binding together the family, it
spreads itself abroad among relations, connections, friends,
and neighbours. Then it includes citizens and those who are
our allies. At last it takes in the whole human race, and that
feeling of the soul arises which, giving every man his own, and
defending by equal laws the rights of each, is called justice.'
It matters little how may have been introduced this great
secret which Christ afterward taught, and for which we look
in vain through the writings of all the philosophers. It comes
here simply from Cicero himself in the midst of his remarks
on the new Academy, but it gives the lesson which had
governed his life: 'I will do unto others as I would they
should do unto me.' In this is contained the rudiments of that

religion which has served to soften the hearts of us all. It is of you I must think, and not of myself.[47]

So the 'true philosophy' turns out to be something Trollope thinks of as religious. His own religious views belong to a certain humanistic Anglican strain that has ties of its own with Cicero, as we shall see. And yet Trollope's study of Cicero provides in itself a solid rational basis for his artistic method. He will take up specific instances with that tender casuistry that best implements Cicero's 'true philosophy'—and his own.

NOTES

[1]Bradford A. Booth has an excellent survey and summary in 'Trollope on the Novel,' *Essays Dedicated to Lily B. Campbell*. Berkeley and Los Angeles, California U.P., 1950, pp. 219–231.

[2]*Autobiography*, p. 191.

[3]L. P. and R. P. Stebbins, *The Trollopes*. New York, AMS Press, Inc., 1945, p. 179.

[4]*Cicero*, i, 261.

[5]A lecture, printed in *Four Lectures*, ed. Morris L. Parrish.

[6]G. Eliot, *Letters*, ed. Gordon S. Haight, iv. New Haven and London, Yale University Press, 1954, 81–82.

[7]*Letters*, ed. Bradford A. Booth. London, Oxford University Press, 1951, p. 266.

[8]'Anthony Trollope and the Classics,' *Classical Weekly*, xxxvii, May 15, 1944, 227–231.

[9]*Cicero*, i, 8, 9, 62, 63 *et passim*.

[10]i, 104.   [11]i, 104, note.   [12]ii, 118.   [13]ii, 130.

[14]See especially i, 21.

[15]i, 22–23. The first tag, *Fiat justitia, ruat caelum*, sometimes *Fiat justitia, pereat mundus*, is obscure in origin, and so common as to be proverbial. The second, *Rem si possis recte . . .* is almost proverbial, but it is also Horace, *Epistolae* i, 1, 65. In Trollope's novels, the references to the two are legion; they are always used to refer to the two opposing moral modes.

[16]ii, 51. Cicero, *Ad. Fam.*, i, 9. Trollope gives his own translation, and sometimes he accompanies it with the Latin. The references are Trollope's, collated by me with the Loeb edition, and none of Trollope's references that I have checked is wrong. In these notes, I give the Loeb reference along with Trollope's. Here, Loeb, p. 78.

[17]ii, 311. *De Legibus*, lib. iii, ca. x; Loeb, p. 484.

[18]I, 270. Other examples, of many, are I, 114; I, 179.

[19]I, 23.

[20]Trollope refers to Mommsen's condemnation of the morals of the age more than once. For example, II, 226–227.

[21]II, 69.   [22]II, 228.   [23]II, 100.

[24]*A Grammar of Motives.* New York, Prentice-Hall, 1945, pp. 503, 512.

[25]*Cicero,* I, 137.   [26]*Cicero,* II, 191. Cf. *Cicero,* I, 23.

[27]II, 127.   [28]I, 15.

[29]But this is not relevant to the epistolatory novel. For in it, the author disappears. Richardson does not address us, but rather we have Pamela addressing her parents, and we read over their shoulders.

[30]Eric Partridge, *Dictionary of Slang and Unconventional English.* New York, Macmillan, and London, Routledge & Kegan Paul, 1961; notes nineteenth-century uses of this as *bluff,* or pretentious swagger. I think it is what we would call a *put-on.*

[31]*Cicero,* I, 37. And then, to make the friendship perfect, Trollope found in Cicero approval of hunting as sport. I do not know if or how hunting is relevant to humane letters, but it is relevant to Trollope.

[32]I, 123.

[33]*The Roman Way.* New York, Norton, 1957, p. 50. It is interesting that in a very casual context, the same classicist records her sense of a fellowship between Cicero and Trollope. 'To pass from Cicero . . . is rather like passing from Archdeacon Grantly and the pleasant people of Barset. . . .' (p. 70).

[34]*Cicero,* I, 185.

[35]II, 323. *Tusc. Disputationes,* lib. 1, ca. xxx; Loeb, p. 86. See also *Cicero* I, 59–60. Here, Trollope notes Cicero's references to the Eleusinian mysteries, *De Legibus,* lib. ii, ca. xiv. What little more we know now of the mysteries bears out Trollope's appreciation of their importance to Cicero. The sacred objects, grain and the phallus, imply the sacredness of life, and consequently the iniquity of suicide.

[36]II, 323. *De Officiis,* lib. 1, ca. xliv; Loeb, p. 162. I give the Latin here as the passage is so particularly important, and then perhaps the reader will be interested to see how Trollope's version has a pithiness of its own. *Omne officium, quod ad conjunctionem hominum et ad societatem tuendam valet, anteponendum est illi officio, quod cognitione et scientia continetur.*

[37]I, 279. *Letter to Quintus,* partially translated by Trollope, pp. 277–282; Loeb, *Ad Fam.,* III, 388–438.

[38]I, 165, note. *Pro Cluentio,* L; Loeb, p. 370.

[39]II, 319. *De Officiis,* lib. ii, ca. xiv; Loeb, p. 220.

[40]I, 8, 34.   [41]II, 279.   [42]II, 288.

[43]II, 279.   [44]II, 290.   [45]II, 277.

[46]See my article '*Cousin Henry:* Trollope's Note from Antiquity,' *NCF,* XXIV, June, 1969, pp. 93–8.

[47]II, 289. *De Finibus,* lib. v, ca. xxiii; Loeb, pp. 466–468.

Chapter IV

THE TRADITION RENEWED

'En somme, la situation c'est de la matière; cela
demande à être traité. . . . C'est une sorte d'oeuvre d'art. . . .'
'Mais non: c'était . . . un devoir. . . . C'était une question
de morale. Oui, tu peux bien rire: de morale.'
Je ne ris pas du tout.

SARTRE, *La Nausée*

TROLLOPE'S *Cicero* holds a very important place in his
work, then; and yet it is only one part of what might be
called his *classicism,* that aspect of him which has hardly
received due investigation. This naïve chronicler of the
ordinary was in truth something of a learned man. To review
his literary interests even in a brief way is to suspect that the
apparent naïveté is really that art that conceals the art. 'No
doubt many a literary artist so conceals his art that readers
do not know there is much art. But they like the books and
read them—not knowing why.' So says Trollope himself,
writing intimately in a letter to his son Henry.[1] His Latin
studies, his reading in the English Renaissance, and his
informed sense of the history of the English novel, all contribute to the art. And in fact, of all Victorian novelists, it is
Trollope who stands most squarely in the stream of literary
humanism. In one way, he is the most Victorian of them all,
the most specific on behaviour and culture; but in a more
important way he is the least dated. His interest centres not
on the great issues that absorbed the intelligentsia of his time,
but rather on matters that are more timeless—the moral
problems of man in relation to society. That his classical
studies were Latin rather than Greek might be expected; of
course Latin was—and is—more available, but anyway
Trollope is temperamentally less attuned to the Greek spirit
of idealism, abstract thought, and the other-worldly than to

the Latin spirit of the pragmatic, the urbane, the decorous, the of-this-world.

If Cicero is the most Roman of prose writers in this sense, the most Roman of poets is Horace, and no poet pleased Trollope more. Edith Hamilton describes Horace's quality in the respect in which he appealed to Trollope, 'spoke' to him and for him—Horace,

> the complete man of the world, with tolerance for all and partisanship for none; able to get on with everyone and at home everywhere, . . . viewing this earthly scene with some detachment—and almost never in a state of mind where a laugh comes hard.[2]

The novels have a multitude of Horatian allusions and quotations. In the moment of *vale* in the *Autobiography* it is to Horace that Trollope turns, quoting

> Singula de nobis anni praedantur euntes;
> Eripuere jocos, venerem, convivia, ludum;
> Tendunt extorquere poëmata.

He gives Conington's translation, but complains of it as 'flat,' and then proceeds to give nothing other than his own. If any poetry could inspire this *prosateur* Trollope to *poëmata* it would have to be Horace.

> Years as they roll cut all our pleasures short;
> Our pleasant mirth, our loves, our wine, our sport.
> And then they stretch their power, and crush at last
> Even the power of singing of the past.[3]

He presents his version modestly enough, without even saying it *is* his own, and certainly not pretending to the Horatian perfection of utterance. But obviously it moved him greatly: *jocos, venerem, convivia, ludum* were what he loved and grieved to give up, and his version covers these categories with some nicety. As for his *poëmata*, if they are taken to be his novels, then *extorquere* would be the very word: the years would have to *wrench*, to *dislocate by main force* the man from his beloved occupation. This autobiographical chapter concludes at last with another of his translations from Horace, as though he felt a sort of piety in getting it down for the record.

> Vixi puellis nuper idoneus,
> Et militavi non sine gloria;
> Nunc arma defunctumque bello
> Barbiton hic paries habebit.[4]

His favourite sport supplies him with a hunting figure to substitute for Horace's military one:

> I've lived about the covert side,
> I've ridden straight, and ridden fast;
> Now breeches, boots, and scarlet pride
> Are but mementoes of the past.[5]

Maybe these Horatian paraphrases are his most intimate statements, especially if glossed with another passage from the *Autobiography*:

> It will not, I trust, be supposed by any reader that I have intended in this so-called autobiography to give a record of my inner life. . . . If the rustle of a woman's petticoat has ever stirred my blood; if a cup of wine has been a joy to me; if I have thought tobacco at midnight in pleasant company to be one of the elements of an earthly paradise; if now and again I have somewhat recklessly fluttered a £5 over a card table;—of what matter is that to any reader? I have betrayed no woman. Wine has brought me to no sorrow,[6]

and so on. This is hardly an alienated Victorian, wracked with doubt and the sickness of the century. Some of the critical condescension to Trollope has sprung from a sense that he did not even play a role in the Age of Doubt and Alienation. But that the spiritual agonies of his youth were severe is abundantly clear from the *Autobiography*—if we are to take agony as value. We must remember, however, that his art did not take its shape in his period of *Sturm und Drang*: he was thirty-seven when he began to write *The Warden*. Trollope the novelist is a man who has come to terms with himself and his culture, partly at least by acquiring the perspective of that very classical culture which was such a satisfaction to him. His world-view is a long view, and has really much in common with that of Horace and of Cicero.

Whenever he speaks of his art he refers to the old Horatian dictum about combining teaching with pleasing, and there is a decorum in this, too. It suits his anti-romantic, anti-Dionysian views. It is such a commonplace that it has been used unthinkingly more often than not, perhaps; but I believe Trollope considered it carefully and found no better aesthetic. It stands, let it be remembered, back at the beginning of the English novel, in Fielding's preface to *Joseph Andrews*, 'instruction or entertainment'; and it is the Fielding tradition that Trollope follows. Trollope's casuistic art does, I believe, give new life to the Horatian purpose, specifically and precisely:

> Aut prodesse . . . aut delectare . . .
> Aut simul et jucunda et idonea dicere vitae.

One need not be overawed by any professionalism in Trollope's classical scholarship. He makes at least one conspicuous mistake: one of his favourite Latin tags he frequently ascribes to Horace, though it is in fact Ovid. '*Video meliora proboque, deteriora sequor!*' cries Medea overcome by her passion for Jason.[7] Trollope usually has it 'I see the better way, but yet I take the worse,' and it is frequent in his work[8] just because it refers to that eternal cross-grainedness of human beings, which is so often his novelistic concern. He states the theme in his *Cicero*, too: 'Men are unable to fathom their own desires, and fail to govern themselves by the wisdom which is at their fingers' ends.'[9] The Ovidian tag is the sort of thing Horace *might* have said, mocking himself; and meantime as a mistake in scholarship it validates Trollope's amateur standing. It is hardly the part of the gentlemen to be correct in all points of learning.

The breadth and discipline of his reading in English alone,

however, might put an academic to shame. Many of his notes and comments are extant and await publication. He perused and annotated no less than two hundred and fifty-seven specimens of the Old Drama. Professors Bradford Booth and Hugh Dick have collected and assessed these annotations[10] which are often of great interest both for themselves and for relevance to Trollope's own writing. Booth, for instance, indicated the astonishing echoes of Marlowe's *Faustus* in *Orley Farm*,[11] and long ago it was observed that *The Fixed Period* seems to owe its plot to *The Old Law* by Massinger and others.[12] It is interesting that in his comments he never falls into the common contemporary romantic fallacy; always he reads the plays as of the theatre, to be performed on a stage, for an audience. I think there is a parallel here to Trollope's sense of his own genre, the novel. Shakespeare was in show business, and Trollope is in the novel business and responsible to his market. His planned programme of drama reading he undertook rather late in his career as a quarrying for plot and character; but early in his life and throughout it he was devoted to the drama and always had on hand, as it were, the great examples. It has been said that no English novel can be written without Shakespearian allusions, but in Trollope they are legion. They are an index no doubt of the particularity of Trollope's intellectual debt to Shakespeare, but also, I think, of his developing powers in the dramatic aspects of the novel: dialogue, dramatic situation and dramatic irony—all these become his special fortes. It may further be noted that a specific interest in the Jacobean drama is aligned with his interest in moral ambiguities. Lady Mason of *Orley Farm* is not very much like Vittoria Corombona of Webster's *White Devil*, granted, but she stands in a similar position. Both have committed crimes and both conduct themselves as though they were innocent. *Orley Farm* might be logically entitled— not *The White Devil*—but something like *The Innocent Criminal*. *The Noble Jilt* is the actual title he gave to his dramatisation of *Can You Forgive Her?* and since 'jilts' are by definition ignoble, this title indicates for Victorians a marked moral anomaly.

Trollope's other particular interest in the English Renaissance is Francis Bacon, and here again the interest is peculiarly moral, and involves the relation of Bacon's character to his works. Trollope's own character Sir Thomas Underwood in *Ralph The Heir* has made a life-long study of Bacon, and his study is relevant to the moral dereliction of Sir Thomas himself and to the political-ethical dilemmas of that novel (see especially Chapter xi). Asa Briggs has observed that Trollope's novels themselves explore 'the nineteenth-century equivalent of the problems of Bacon's Essays,'[13] and Michael Sadleir has given us Trollope's actual margin notes on the *Essays*.[14]

It is very clear to Trollope that Bacon in general leans much too far away from *honestum* towards *utile*. Where Trollope compares Bacon with Cicero (in the passage quoted above Chapter iii) it is to declare Cicero's moral superiority on this point, and the general tenor of Trollope's comments on the *Essays* shows something very like disgust with this ethic of expediency.

Trollope's fascination with Bacon lies in what he feels as an enigma: Bacon had a mind as distinguished as Cicero's, a similar social-political engagement, and moreover, a similar philosophical attitude; and yet the *Novum Organum* availed him nothing in essential virtue. The method, the Novum Organum, is actually to natural phenomena just what Trollope's casuistry is to human phenomena. The abstraction, the syllogism, is for Bacon 'no match for the subtlety of nature,' and we must proceed by experiment. Where Bacon indicts the 'Idols of the Theatre,' he indicts the very principles of systematic philosophy that both Cicero and Trollope deplore.

> Neither do I mean this only of entire systems, but also of many principles and axioms. . . . I maintain a sort of suspension of judgement. . . . We must entreat man again and

again to discard, or at least set apart for a while these volatile
and preposterous philosophies, which have preferred theses
to hypotheses, led experience captive, and triumphed over
the works of God.[15]

Experience in Trollope's novels is to be supreme; his novels
apply Bacon's inductive method. Trollope's cases parallel
Bacon's experiments. And Bacon's own case is one which
would have demonstrated for Trollope the overriding urgency
of moral philosophy. Trollope would again insist with Cicero
that 'All duty which tends to protect the society of man with
men is to be preferred to that of which science is the simple
object.'[16] The Baconian-Lucretian 'vantage ground of Truth'
is a vantage ground for art as well as for science. It is the
ground of the spectators in the theatre, and in ironic fiction
it is the ground shared by the narrator and his reader. And
it is this kind of fiction, I suggest, which constitutes the
literary-humanistic school to which Trollope belongs. He was,
I should say, eminently aware of it as a tradition. His plan to
write a history of the novel in English was not carried out
(though as he tells in his *Autobiography* he did some laborious
reading for it), but the fact that he had such a plan is a mark
of his literary art-consciousness. Even George Eliot, who may
be respected as an intellectual more than Trollope, does not
have Trollope's sense of literary tradition.

Cervantes makes a convenient starting-point for considering the relevance of the tradition in question, because he is
highly literary—his novel is *about* novels among other things
—and because both Fielding and Sterne are much supported
by his example. Of course Trollope knew him, as everyone
does, but the concept of quixotism turns up in his work with
fairly remarkable frequency. Plantagenet Palliser in his stubborn virtue is typically quixotic, and the American Senator
(in the last chapter of the novel named for him) is pointedly
compared to the Don himself. Then there is something in
Trollope's method very like Cervantes': does not the Don
start out as an absurd caricature, and proceed to take on

light and shade? and as he becomes real is he not more and more surrounded with the author's tenderness, and a kind of blessing? In a slighter way, the Signora Vesey-Neroni in *Barchester Towers* follows this pattern, and, as Trollope's art develops, the pattern is repeated with countless other characters. The most obvious aspect of Cervantes' irony is, of course, the deflation of romance by means of realism, and this too is Trollope's theme in countless variations.

It is Fielding and Sterne who take up the Cervantes strain in English—Defoe with his *roman-vérité*, Richardson and Smollett with their epistles and their picaros—all stand outside this ironic tradition, perhaps because they defect as narrators. With Fielding most especially, the narrator is a palpable presence and an audible voice. One of Trollope's best readers, Chauncey Brewster Tinker, notes the kinship with Trollope: 'Not even Henry Fielding associates with his readers on more agreeable terms. . . . [Trollope] is charitable and broad-minded, and it is a privilege to be with him.'[17]

The concept of the gentleman, so often declared to be very important in Victorian times—declared to be so but not explained *how* so—functions similarly in the work of Fielding and Trollope. Of course one reason why it has not been explained, is that it is not seemly for a gentleman to explain it—Trollope carefully and pointedly omits the explanation in his *Autobiography*, just where it is logically needed (in Chapter III). The vulgar cannot explain it, and twentieth-century liberals of course find the concept either absurd or unpalatable, with its assumptions of class. But it is nevertheless a moral ideal. Cicero, not being English, and neither vulgar nor liberal, could explain about it, and *did*, in the *De Officiis*; and as Edith Hamilton says, it is Cicero who promulgated the ideal in English schools in the old rotten days of stratified education. William Empson has a clear-sighted little essay on *Tom Jones* where he faces the issue; he says Fielding could have defined gentleman literally enough: 'He means by it a person fit to sit on the bench as a magistrate, and naturally such a man needs to know all about the people he is to judge.'[18] Just so does Trollope feel sure the gentleman makes the best civil servant, because of the qualities of uprightness and breadth of understanding, which he does define—not where he discusses the Civil Service in the *Autobiography* but where he explicates *honestum* in the *Cicero*. It is interesting that both Fielding and Trollope worked in the public service, and might be supposed to know therefore more of the problems of practical ethics, both public and private. What Fielding and Trollope do is to teach the lessons of *honestum* by the method of ironic narration. Fielding, says Empson, puts across a relativistic idea, and 'he does not find relativism alarming, because he feels that to understand other codes than your own is likely to make your judgments better.'[19] Sharing Fielding's vantage ground, we see around characters and moral problems and appreciate the incongruous way of things. We see how a selfish motive can have a good result, and often enough, God knows, we see Tom's generous impulse result in a wrong. Or we see how appearances can deceive; the contrast between Blifil and Tom hinges on the contrasts of *seems* and *is*, and our superior knowledge. Above all, we do not suffer with Fielding—or with Trollope—from what Empson calls 'the view of Flaubert, Conrad and so forth, that a novelist is positively not allowed to discuss the point of the novel.'[20]

The great common ground of Fielding and Sterne, so dissimilar in general tenor, is that both extend ironic friendships to the reader. Sterne probably achieves the most intimate relationship of this sort ever achieved, and exploits it with the most extravagant virtuosity. Remember only, 'As you proceed further with me, the slight acquaintance which is now beginning betwixt us, will grow into familiarity; and that, unless one of us is in fault, will terminate in friendship.' The fact that the friendship between Sterne and Trollope himself could not be perfect must not make us overlook similarities in their methods. Certainly it could not be perfect.

Trollope would not recommend the frankness of any of the eighteenth century novelists, and Smollett's saltiness and Sterne's snigger are more offensive to him by far than Fielding's heartiness. (But Miss Marrable, a perfect lady in *The Vicar of Bullhampton*, has a taste for Smollett, and even for Wycherley! IX.) A moral relativity like Trollope's is demonstrated by such things as Uncle Toby's charity to the fly: the best of moral principles is reduced to an exquisite absurdity. The most searching realism, and with Sterne the realism is especially a realism of psychological processes, is the means to the appreciation of the complications of ethics. As A. E. Dyson observes when he comes to consider Sterne's irony, Sterne's people are 'simply kindly people, for all their strange psychologies,' and Sterne proclaims the 'grand simple decencies' beneath all.[21] I think most readers would agree that Trollope beats Sterne on the grand simple decencies. I would like to insist too, however, that he is like Sterne in his interest in the strange psychologies, the mixed and confused motives that are the springs of action in ourselves whom we consider sometimes to be so logical. The eighteenth century was a fine time to deflate the pretensions of rationality; but Trollope's time was perhaps equally good. Utilitarians and perfectibilians were abroad, and other sensible systematisers. Both Sterne and Trollope were exploring odd evidence behind the most ordinary surfaces, and suspending judgment in matters of morals, just as Bacon has had us do in science.

With Jane Austen we come very much closer to Trollope; early, he decided *Pride and Prejudice* was the best novel in the English language.[22] Though he later modified that judgment he did not essentially change it. Certainly Trollope early appreciated and admired Jane Austen's ability to hold in suspension the multiple views of things, and the artistic control that comes from this, and the wit that comes only with the control. Mary Lascelles has a fine phrase for it in her study of Jane Austen; she calls it 'the instant perception of the absurd,'[23] that same kind of quick humour noted in

Cicero and in Horace, in Cervantes and Fielding and Sterne. It is also the humour of Trollope, who will not permit a pretension, an incongruity, or a discrepancy to get by, without discovering it to us and surprising us into a laugh.

There are many specific technical parallels between Jane Austen and Trollope. Jane Austen makes much use of indirect discourse, and actually the same is true of Trollope, although it has not been much noted.[24] Both often use it even for important and focal remarks. This may seem a strange fact in artists who have such flair for dramatic dialogue. But oddly enough indirect discourse can achieve something the direct discourse of the drama cannot do. It can help the ironic author keep his firm control over his material and over the reader's attitude to the material. It indicates how we are to consider this remark or that; it is slanted reporting. In this way it reinforces the aesthetic distancing, and the artist's control. It can be a very condensed and deft sort of technique, as indeed it is with Jane Austen and with both Thackeray and Trollope as well.

But if we give our attention to the larger ironies that shape these matters of style, we see still more striking similarities between Jane Austen and Trollope. 'The more I see of the world,' says Elizabeth in *Pride and Prejudice*, 'the more I am dissatisfied with it; and every day confirms my belief of the inconsistency of all human characters, and of the little dependence that can be placed on the appearance of either merit or sense.' This is surely a Trollopian text. Both Jane Austen and Trollope teach us to embrace the very inconsistency. There is a difference in degree: I think Jane Austen assumes more rationality in behaviour than Trollope does, and I think Trollope embraces the absurd more lovingly. Certainly he explores at a more leisurely pace, in a more discursive fashion, and moves wider and deeper. No one would want to make a value judgment here: Jane Austen is merely perfect. As Edmund Gosse said, 'Unfortunately, other novelists were not so sequestered.' But unquestionably

Trollope has more to say. The point is only that the process is the same: the display of incongruities and the achievement of moral perceptions. Trollope learned from her the interdependency of good and evil, and saw her strong moral purpose: 'The faults of some [of her characters] are the anvils on which the virtues of others are hammered till they are bright as steel.' The passage continues: 'In the comedy of folly I know no novelist who has beaten her. The letters of Mr. Collins . . . would move laughter in a low-church archbishop. Throughout all her works, and they are not many, a sweet lesson of homely household womanly virtue is ever being taught.'[25] It is noteworthy that Trollope's assertion of her moral office follows close on his declaration of her excellence as humorist. There is, I would say, a close connection. I think his reading of her is still the right one. She is far from being the mocking immoralist some theorists have been so far carried away as to call her.

Trollope partially withdrew the palm from Jane Austen, he tells us, first for Scott, and then for Thackeray.[26] To cede Jane Austen for Scott may shock sensibilities now. But the shock may be mitigated if we think of—say—Jeanie and Effie Deans, and of the depth of character portrayal and moral grandeur of which Scott was capable. How could a 'novelist of character' like Trollope withhold his admiration? He knew how bad Scott is at his worst, in those endless *longueurs*; he himself wrote: 'Scott seems to have understood well not only that Homer might nod sometimes, but that if he could only wake up upon occasion he might spend much of his time in sleep.'[27] The long dreary stretches just do not cancel out the excellences of Scott.

With Thackeray we come closest to Trollope; he is the one whom Trollope placed without question at the head of the novelists of his own age. His critiques of Thackeray are always revealing just because the two are so close in artistic interest; where he praises Thackeray we can often tell where he himself was aiming; where he dispraises, we can guess what tendencies he wanted to check in himself. Thackeray has been the prime example of 'irony' in the Victorian novel, for a long time. And for the kind of irony that is an instrument of satire, of scorn, of cynicism, he *is* the prime example—but he is also much more than this. He himself felt that his critics over-emphasised his cynicism, and we could feel so too. Yet the negative qualities are strong. The concept of the Snob does after all extend itself to condemn just about the whole world of humanity. And the great theme of his greatest book is a negative theme. *Vanity Fair* is a bitter spectacle that takes in a very wide range of human life.

But this is not all there is to Thackeray's irony, and for the rest he is very like in kind to Trollope. He is conspicuously the omniscient author-friend, most successfully so in *Vanity Fair*. He plays on the relationship, with, I think it is agreed, emi-nent success. His pretence as showman or puppeteer succeeds delightfully just because Becky and her crowd do not jerk or limp puppet-wise, at all, but are so real as to seem to turn around of their own force. We see them do so, and then when Thackeray reminds us of the puppet proscenium arch, he reinforces the whole framework of irony, and we see, even in the playfulness of the scheme, something of the dark Necessity behind human affairs. As dramatic ironist, what fine capital he makes out of such scenes as the great ball before Waterloo. How much the richer the situations are for our shared superior knowledge then; and thereafter for Becky's and our own superior knowledge of the dead and canonised George.

He is most especially like Trollope in his alertness to moral ironies, such things as the good qualities of Becky the Bad and the sins of Amelia the Good. On this aspect of Thackeray's irony, A. E. Dyson has some penetrating remarks that would apply even better to Trollope.

> In extending our understanding and compassion, Thackeray does the work a novelist is chiefly concerned to do. . . .
> Mr. Osborne's selfishness and tyranny are strongly realised, yet his suffering when George dies is none the less powerful

and real. Thackeray is able to make us feel pity for a man like ourselves even as we probe the bitter impurities of grief.[28]

Trollope probes these bitter impurities even in so good-hearted a grief as that of Archdeacon Grantly for his dying father, or he makes us feel pity even for a scoundrel like Ferdinand Lopez. Trollope is much concerned to note in Thackeray this power to reach through to compassion. He admires such creations as Colonel Newcome, inasmuch as Thackeray could, Trollope writes, 'force us to love him, a weak and silly old man.'[29] Even such a snob as Major Pendennis at the end clutches our sympathy. Trollope surveys Thackeray's whole achievement in these words:

> . . . he has taken upon himself the special task of barking at the vices and follies of the world around him. . . . He was 'crying his sermon,' hoping, if it might be so, to do something towards lessening the evils he saw around him. . . . He had become so urgent in the cause, so loud in his denunciations, that he did not stop often to speak of the good things around him. Now and again he paused and blessed amid the torrent of his anathemas.[30]

It was important for Trollope to note this act of blessing, for it is much more characteristic of Trollope than of Thackeray, and proceeds, I submit, from a larger ironic view, a larger perspective of perspectives, and an acceptance of things. It seems to me that Trollope's irony is more controlling, if also more humane:

In some respects, Thackeray markedly fails in artistic control. First, he was a man *gêné* by Victorian conventions, witness the well-known preface to *Pendennis*, and the well-known failure of *Pendennis* as compared with *Tom Jones*. Trollope, I hope to show, did not find that the conventions hampered his art; rather, they are themselves part of his material, and he turns them to his advantage. This whole matter is vital to irony, for one condition of irony must be a certain free play of mind. Thackeray often just cannot say what he wants to say, and then he cannot be quite honest; he turns arch and mannered, and the ironic author-friend relationship is strained. Trollope notes the strain: 'his most besetting sin . . . is a certain affected familiarity. . . . [when this occurs] The book is robbed of its integrity.'[31] A more serious failure in irony lies, I think, in his inability to sustain detachment. Professor Gordon Ray has shown that much of Thackeray's own love-life, its frustrations and vengeance, is played out in his books, especially in *Henry Esmond*.[32] This makes *Henry Esmond* an 'uncomfortable book' as George Eliot said,[33] and even 'unsavoury' as Frederic Harrison said.[34] If so distinguished an artist can be said to have a great flaw, it is this: his proper, chosen mode is irony, and he fails in ironic detachment. It is a curious phenomenon, artistic irony, how it demands detachment as a condition for the achievement of that least detached of things — compassion.

In general, Thackeray and Trollope are certainly the most closely related of the Victorian novelists, and their common ground consists in, for the most part, the ironic temper. In both, this is connected to their humanistic traditionalism, their sense of the long continuity of literary culture. In contrast, George Eliot has stronger ties with philosophy and social science than with literary tradition, and Dickens with the fairy tale and popular spectacle. Both Thackeray and Trollope are grounded in Ciceronian *honestum*, both are informed, urbane, and both great humorists of the ironic sort. It might be said that they are the most classical of the Victorians. But the differences in classicism are important. Thackeray has a great nostalgia for the English Augustan age, and tries to emulate it. Trollope has none of this nostalgia, but is rather most heartily in and of his time. When Thackeray aims to be Augustan he often unfortunately latches on to the sentimentality of 'Dick' Steele. Trollope is more his own man, and does in truth seem to be his own Augustan.[35] So, while Thackeray has great achievements in ironic art to his credit, achievements of a sort occasionally grander than Trollope's,

Trollope stands on more secure ground, which affords him the firmer perspective and the more consistent success.

NOTES

[1] *Letters*, p. 386.

[2] *The Roman Way*, p. 88.

[3] *Autobiography*, p. 292; Horace, *Epistles*, 2, 2, 55–57; Loeb, p. 428.

[4] *Odes*, 3, 26; Loeb, p. 260.

[5] *Autobiography*, p. 292.

[6] P. 304.

[7] *Metamorphoses*, VII, 11, 20–21.

[8] A few of many instances: *Four Lectures*, p. 86; *The Prime Minister*, LXVII; *Ayala's Angel*, XXXVIII.

[9] *Cicero*, I, 286.

[10] In the unpublished *Trollope on the Old Drama*. I am indebted to the late Professor Booth for the opportunity to read this.

[11] Trollope's '*Orley Farm:* Artistry *Manqué*,' *From Jane Austen to Joseph Conrad*, eds. R. C. Rathburn and Martin Steinmann. Minneapolis, University of Minnesota Press, 1958, pp. 160–176.

[12] B. A. Booth, *Anthony Trollope*. Indiana, Indiana University Press, 1958, p. 129. London, E. Hulton & Co. Ltd.

[13] *Victorian People*. London, Odhams Press, 1954, and New York, Harper & Row, 1963, p. 107. Also Penguin Books, Harmondsworth, 1970.

[14] "Trollope and Bacon's Essays,' *NCF* (then, *The Trollopian*), I, Summer, 1945, 21–34.

[15] *Magna Instauratio* in *Essays . . .*, ed. R. F. Jones. New York, 1937, pp. 280, 330, 369. I do not know that Bacon's own debts to Cicero have been investigated. Especially striking is the similarity of the Idols-of-the-Forum idea to Cicero's linguistic concepts. See, for instance, *Academica*, II, xlvi.

[16] See Chapter III, note 36; *Cicero* II, 323; *De Officiis*, lib. 1, ca. xliv; Loeb, p. 162.

[17] "Trollope,' *Essays in Retrospect*. New Haven, Yale University Press, 1948 pp. 114, 116.

[18] "Tom Jones,' *Kenyon Review*, XX, Spring, 1958, p. 249.

[19] P. 231.   [20] P. 236.

[21] *The Crazy Fabric*. London, Macmillan, and New York, St. Martin's Press, 1965, p. 47.

[22] *Autobiography*, p. 35.

[23] *Jane Austen and Her Art*. London, Oxford University Press, 1939, p. 106.

[24] David Aitkin remarks it, however, in his study of Trollope's style: 'A Kind of Felicity . . .,' *NCF*, XX, March, 1966, p. 105.

[25]'English Prose Fiction as a Rational Amusement,' *Four Lectures*, p. 105.

[26]*Autobiography*, p. 35.

[27]Quoted, Bradford A. Booth, 'Trollope on Scott: Some Unpublished Notes,' *NCF*, v, December, 1950, 226.

[28]*The Crazy Fabric*, p. 291.

[29]*Autobiography*, p. 203.

[30]*Thackeray*, pp. 203–205.

[31]P. 198.

[32]*Thackeray: The Age of Wisdom.* New York, McGraw-Hill, 1958, pp. 180 ff.

[33]*Letters*, ed. Gordon S. Haight. New Haven, Yale University Press, 1954, II, 67.

[34]Quoted by John E. Tilford, Jr., in 'The "Unsavoury Plot" of *Henry Esmond*,' *NCF*, VI, September, 1951, 121.

[35]A perceptive discussion of this quality is C. J. Vincent's 'Trollope: A Victorian Augustan,' *Queen's Quarterly*, LII, Winter, 1945–1946, 415–428.

Chapter V

THE NOVELIST AS ANGLICAN

Less certainty, more scope.
ROSE MACAULAY

ONE can say either that Trollope's views developed out of his Anglicanism or that he found in Anglicanism a certain support for these views. At any rate, the Anglican Church suits him perfectly. It is a church committed from the start, one might say, to a Situation Ethics, the first insistent and demanding situation being the need of Henry VIII for a divorce. Out of this casuistic beginning there grew, nevertheless, a serviceable church. When it still stood on a ticklish footing, it had the good fortune to be defined by such saintly worthies as Whitgift and Hooker. Its rationale reflects Elizabeth's respect for the privacy of conscience of her subjects; and it was under the aegis of Hooker's *Laws of Ecclesiastical Polity* and its rather permissive doctrine that the church became established actually as it was legally. From the beginning it has been a church inclined to tolerant casuistry rather than the Letter of the Law—a Trollopian, an existentialist church. It kept within its fold such as John Wesley, with his strong vocation to go out into the fields and savannahs, and such as Sidney Smith, who found his vocation to consist in dining out. It embraces Dean Arabin and Obadiah Slope, the Red Dean of Canterbury and T. S. Eliot, and the 'heretical' Bishop Pike of California, along with many parsons just as fundamentalist as a Bible Belt Baptist. Shane Leslie, who 'went over to Rome,' and is something of a connoisseur of churches, writes that 'The ideal of the English Church has been to provide a resident gentleman for every parish in the Kingdom, and there have been worse ideals.'[1] It is the most convenient church for a Ciceronian gentleman. It ingratiates itself with humane letters in having provided two great monuments: the official monument of the King James Bible, and through the communal efforts of innumerable clergymen the unofficial monument of the Oxford English Dictionary. It is a refuge for those who do not care to concern themselves with doctrine. When Sartre writes of his own protestant background in the Schweitzer family, he might be writing of Anglican society: 'La Bonne Société croyait en Dieu pour ne pas parler de Lui.'[2] In the house of Archdeacon Grantly, to open a discussion of Ultimate Reality would hardly be good manners.

The Church's extreme permissiveness—or doctrinal caginess—has of course been even notorious. One of the prettiest satires comes in Osbert Sitwell's *Miracle on Sinai*.[3] A very carefully selected group of tourists make a picnic expedition up Mount Sinai, and as luck would have it a new Decalogue is revealed, and the revelation is so momentary that not one of them has time to read it all through, let alone record it. The picnickers, therefore, try to piece it together from imperfect memory, which turns out to be wishful memory. The devoted member of the Royal Society for the Prevention of Cruelty to Animals is sure that she saw BE KIND TO ANIMALS, and so on. When the Anglican Bishop tries to remember what he saw, all he can be sure of, all he can commit himself to having indubitably seen and known and been convinced of is this one precept: SAFETY FIRST. This is, of course, the only piece of doctrine that could not possibly offend any part or party of the Anglican Church. It is as far as he dare go.

You can even make a negative case for the Church of England, as Rose Macaulay's Greek student does in *The Towers of Trebizond*.[4] He did not care to be a Moslem, as the Moslem Turks had been less than kind to the Greeks; and 'The Greek papas were so extremely backward, and Roman Catholics were known to be idolatrous, and Seventh-Day Adventists insane, and American Baptists talked too much.'[5] Rose Macaulay, however, behind the persona of her rather breathless narrator, is clear enough on the positive side. 'Anglicans have less certainty but more scope,'[6] and furthermore the very permissiveness and variety is not at all one of the scandals of the Church ('though there are plenty of these'); its comprehensiveness is its glory.[7]

The great doctrinal storms of the nineteenth century effected rediscovery, redefinitions, and reappraisal of the Via Media in its essential comprehensiveness. The extremes of evangelicalism and of the Oxford Movement forced acceptance of the Middle Way as in actuality the Many Ways. Not quite the Any Way, but nearly. Hamilton, Bishop of Salisbury, observed at the time of *Essays and Reviews*, 'However comprehensive may be the limits within which our tolerant Church allows her clergy to exercise their ministry, those limits must exist somewhere.'[8] So he believed, but his querulous note suggests that contemporary controversy was extending these limits to the disappearing point.

Can such a delimited entity be said to have a rationale or an artistic product? We know well that the Oxford Movement has; and we know also that the Evangelical movement has its literary propaganda and its historical significance. Its literary results perhaps take their best form as reaction: the poetry of doubt and alienation largely presupposes an antecedent evangelical literalism. But there *is* also a philosophy of the Via Media: that neglected strain of thinking called Intuitionism; if it has an artistic correlative, perhaps Trollope's novels make the best example. Jerome Schneewind has drawn attention to the importance of Intuitionism as a school and as an influence. 'Thanks to J. S. Mill,' he says, 'everyone is familiar with the utilitarian position on the issues, but the Intuitionist standpoint is, quite surprisingly considering its importance for the thought of the period, almost completely neglected in histories of philosophy no less than in surveys of literature.'[9] We all know it in its popular form, in the commonplace Victorian concept of Conscience and the still small voice. But it had then as now a conceptual validity. It is the assumption, for instance, in the passage on ethics by Bertrand Russell quoted above in Chapter II. Schneewind indicates its nineteenth-century rationale by reference to William Whewell, John Grote, and James Martineau. Of these, Whewell and Grote were both typical high Anglican divines; Martineau was a Unitarian, but very close in thinking to this kind of Anglicanism. Schneewind might well have added F. D. Maurice to his references, but of course Schneewind's interest is more philosophy proper and Maurice belongs more to theology proper; though in this case, neither is very proper— Intuitionism slips over easily into 'moral-philosophy'-theology, and the religious idea of Conscience has a philosophical base in Intuitionism.

Whewell, Grote, and Maurice in themselves demonstrate the philosophical base of the nineteenth-century Via Media, which on the one hand returns to and revitalises the original Anglican thinking of the seventeenth century, and on the other hand anticipates what is most vital in twentieth-century Anglicanism, the newly stated intuitionist moral philosophy made current by contemporary Anglican apologists. The Church of England has in fact a right to feel a proprietary interest in Situation Ethics; though the French existentialists do autonomously exercise what they call 'morale de situation.'

Whewell, Grote, and above all Maurice, are involved as thinkers in a special way with Anglican casuistry, and also by a curious circumstance with the actual term. It all starts with the death in 1677 of John Knightsbridge, scholar and divine, rector of Spofforth in Yorkshire, who left by his will fifty pounds annually to Cambridge to 'a professor of moral theology or casuistical divinity.' The first election to the chair, called the Knightsbridge Professorship, was made in 1683. Knightsbridge stands in a position somewhat like Hiram's in *The Warden* insofar as he and the changing times worked together to create an anomaly that would in itself be an excellent donnée for another Trollopian novel. What do you *do* with an ancient endowment for a professor of Casuistry, when it's questionable whether the subject is a discipline at all, and even if it is, it's in bad odour. It's like having a Professor of Equivocation, or Double-Think.[10] The term casuistry had even in Knightsbridge's day a contemptuous sense, equalling *sophistry* or *jesuitry*; but its concomitant technical 'clean' sense was stronger then than now. Moral Theology (or Ethics) lent itself to three methods: first and oldest, the patristic; second and medieval, the scholastic; third and modern (modern meaning c. 1550 ff.), the *casuistic*.[11] *Casuistique* in French, old and new, remains fairly free of the contemptuous flavour: Englishmen might suppose the French do not even know when they are being jesuitical. The OED gives the present technical sense of casuistry as 'that part of Ethics which resolves cases of conscience, applying the general rules of religion and morality to particular instances in which "circumstances alter cases," or in which there appears to be a conflict of duties.' Anyway, there was a chair of it at Cambridge, and for a long time it was a sinecure. In 1838, however, William Whewell was elected to the Knightsbridge Professorship and took it seriously. He was one of those who looked back to seventeenth-century Anglicanism and the illustrious exponents of casuistry contemporary with Knightsbridge. One is Jeremy Taylor, whose great contribution to the field is his *Ductor Dubitantium* (1660), called 'a compendium of casuistry . . . intended to guide the Anglican clergy in the practice of confession.' Another is Robert Sanderson, Bishop of Lincoln, whose *Nine Cases of Conscience Occasionally Determined* (1678) was edited and commented on by our William Whewell in 1851. Whewell illustrates the connection between old-fashioned Casuistry and new-fashioned Intuitionism in that both assume that we 'intuit the moral quality of particular instances.'[12] John Grote succeeded Whewell in the Knightsbridge Professorship in 1855, a man like Whewell in piety and learning, and perhaps still more distinguished intellectually. It was he who saw clearly that Utilitarianism must be ultimately deterministic while any rationale for ethics must assume both free will and intuition.[13] He is believed to have coined the word *relativism*[14] which in itself proclaims his kind of casuistic thinking.[15] (It was apparently Coleridge in his function as antennae of the race who had already given us *relativity*. See O E D.)

During the incumbencies of both Whewell and Grote, the office seems to have been referred to as the 'Knightsbridge Professorship of Moral Philosophy,' or 'Moral Theology,' interchangeably, the word *casuistry* being apparently avoided on purpose. But when on the death of Grote in 1866, F. D. Maurice was elected, he revived the old title: 'Knightsbridge Professorship of Casuistry, Moral Theology and Moral Philosophy'; his inaugural lecture was 'Casuistry, Moral Philosophy and Moral Theology,' and in 1868 he published *The Conscience, Lectures on Casuistry* in which he defines and defends the word and the concept in a way highly significant for the thought of the time, and incidentally relevant both by implication and by explanation, to the art of the novel.

Maurice is occasionally obscure, and occasionally remote in taste: he *will* admire Holman Hunt's painting 'The Awakened Conscience.' But his sense of language as revelatory of psychic processes, and his psyche-centred attitudes are not at all remote. The first two lectures 'On the Word *I*' and 'On the Word *Conscience*' offer typical samples. He acclaims Socrates' *egotism*, which consists in *Know thyself*, and there is no better way to *know* than through language. Egotism is the means to the realisation of the *I*, essential in that it is only by that realisation we can achieve the sense of other *I*'s. We have the words *consciousness* and *conscience* because we are *I*'s; and our words *ought* and *ought not* in themselves reveal *conscience* as a real entity. *Conscience* 'is emphatically the witness of a supremacy over me directly, not over me as one of the atoms of which the world is composed. I do not proceed from the world to myself; but from myself to the world. I know of its governor only so far as I know of mine.'[16] He pleads for *egotism* 'that each of us may reverence his own life and the life of his fellow man above all theories.'[17] Rules are not adequate for morality: they are like the rules of grammar in that we must devote study to the exceptions. He reveres Socrates for his anti-systematism, and indeed Maurice is so emphatic on this point that he was known for his 'system-phobia.'[18] With system he puts Utilitarianism, determinism, and churches that are doctrinally rigid; and he acclaims the Anglican church for its lack of system. He insists that any systematisation of ethics denies us our free will. And the method of non-system is—Casuistry.

The last of these lectures is 'The Office of the Casuist in the Modern World.' He defends again his use of the word, because we need the thing:

> I have adhered in this instance to the language of the 17th century because I consider it the best language for the 19th century, because I think Casuistry is even more wanted for the England of our days than for the England of any previous day. . . . I adhere strictly to the original sense of the word. It always meant the study of Cases of Conscience. That is what I mean by it. . . . Casuistry is the right introduction to Moral Philosophy.[19]

He goes on to take up the contemporary art of the novel.[20] Even though in previous times 'a novelist like Fielding had a very remarkable insight into many of the deceptions which men practise on themselves, as well as with some of their better impulses,' the best of our novelists now go far beyond this in critical analysis of psychologies. They do it best when they speak as individuals themselves: 'it is good that a man should be recognised as a being and not merely as a speaker; as having spoken out something of his own very self. . . . Our age loves Personality.' (*Our* age collates this with Wayne Booth's strictures against the ultimate immorality of impersonal narration. Our age might further relate the *I–Thou* ethical principles of Martin Buber to the principle of the novelist as *I*.) It is good to have the author as personality for it is as an *I* that he make the case relate to the *I* who reads, just as the prophet Nathan to King David: 'Thou art the man.' *This* is the office of the Casuist. Accordingly when Thackeray addresses the reader he is saying 'Thou art the man'; 'Judge not that ye be not judged.' The Casuist warns us 'against the quackery of . . . prescriptions.' The Casuist warns us against declaring ourselves altogether evil, for he insists on complexity which is to insist on the good in man, on Conscience, and free will. 'The subject which he speaks of is a subject for books only because it is a subject for men and women.' 'You cannot contemplate the individual man out of Society,' for Society consists of '*I*'s.' The casuist is to investigate the relations in which the Persons stand to each other. And this means: Begin with Casuistry. 'No theory ought to occupy us except so far as it is an interpretation of facts. The facts must come first.' (Existence precedes essence?)

Maurice says he rejoices to belong to a country where philosophy gives precedence to Politics. For 'I believe the soundest Moral Science will be that which is demanded by the necessities of a Practical Politics. . . . The moralist never maintains his own position so well as when he asserts the highest dignity for the Politician.'

This seems to me a worthy rationale and an apt one for the novels of Trollope. Maurice himself complains of Thackeray's 'manner,' and says he functions as casuist in spite of it. Trollope—whom Maurice does not mention—surely best fulfils the programme for the novelist as casuist, even to the extension into politics. He speaks to us as author with the most directness and least manner, best relating the case to the reader. He is passionate against system, and passionate for the precedence of the *I*, as his situation-structure demonstrates. He says to us 'Thou art the man'; though his version is often closer to Horace's laughing one: 'De te, fabula!'[21] It is an *Anglican* programme for the novel, not Evangelical-Anglican, nor Anglo-Catholic-Anglican, but that mid-stream old High anti-dogmatic practical Anglican, so cautious on doctrine as to be suspiciously non-committal, but yet redeemed from Laodiceanism by the virtue of its exemplars. Men like Whewell, Grote and Maurice looked back to their seventeenth-century prototypes, and in redefining or re-undefining their church recovered some of its old virtue. No one can read Walton's *Lives* (Donne, Wooten, Hooker, Herbert and Sanderson) and be unmoved by what is a special kind of Anglican saintliness, Walton's own as well as his subjects. Dean Burgon's *Lives of Twelve Good Men* (London, 1888) is not altogether unworthy as a latter-day Walton. Burgon's twelve are not such great men as Walton's five, and Burgon runs to two long-winded Victorian volumes, almost a thousand pages. But his subjects, all High Anglicans, are full of humane grace—learning and wit and piety.

Trollope is our only Anglican novelist in this sense, except possibly Fielding. (And Parson Adams is obviously of the same church as Harding and Grantly.) Certainly no Victorian novelist of any stature can stand with him as a Maurice-style casuist. Thackeray is on the one hand too sentimental and on the other too ill at ease with convention. One feels Dickens comes from that class level that had no religion, and religion in his novels is part of his show, part of his superb theatricalism. George Eliot never escaped her Evangelical origins, but was always functioning in reaction. Of course she came round to placing a value on the Church as convention, and loves her High Anglicans like Mr. Irwine in *Adam Bede*; but she could never be quite at ease with the vagueness of High Anglicanism, and lusted, I think, after System.

This High Anglican Church is acquainted with Politics. The very fact of Establishment forces it into casuistry, not always in Maurice's good sense, but sometimes so. We of course feel that this expediency is at odds with religion, and people like Trollope believed that this feeling would win out, and that Disestablishment was bound to come, as the novel *Phineas Redux* implies. The issue shifted, however, and the Church stayed established mostly because of indifference. What strength is has now lies, interestingly enough, in the revitalising of this main-stream casuistry and in the value of tradition as such—anywhere, that is, but in what Maurice abhorred as 'System.' An Established Church is at the very least a social convenience. Our poor presidents in America are obliged to take on ecumenicism with office and to rush about to masses, meetings, services and fellowships. At state occasions when we want the grandeur of a ceremonial respect paid to a force not ourselves that makes for righteousness, we must rotate the office with elaborate fairness among rabbi, priest, minister and Unitarian. Meantime we have in our heritage a body of literature written out of an ecclesiastical position secure in its flexibility, strong in tradition, a support to political honesty, and also as I think a support to novelistic honesty.

A Christianity that accepts the pagan Cicero as virtually Christian may seem too broad to be anything at all. But Trollope is not unique in his view of Cicero as something like Christian: Saint Augustine himself tells us it was Cicero who first aroused him to a desire for that wisdom that was to lead him eventually to God.[22] And of all kinds of professed Christianity it is this Intuitionistic ethics that is most clearly related to Cicero. The *De Officiis* is in fact Cicero's collection of 'Cases of Conscience,' and its importance in English education brought Cicero very close to the Anglican tradition. Finally, Trollope says:

> Read Cicero's works through from the beginning to the end, and you shall feel that you are living with a man whom you might accompany across the village green to church, should he be kind enough to stay with you over the Sunday. The urbanity, the softness, the humanity, the sweetness are all there.[23]

High Anglicans will not be at all surprised to find urbanity so close to godliness. This certainly is a religion of Intuitionism; and matters of doctrine, of System or 'belief' are hardly of much moment.

To tell the whole truth, the concept of 'belief' is something

71582

of an illusion, Trollope himself would say. He is radically sceptical even as to the underlying thought processes generally assumed. Repeatedly in the novels he uses the remarkable locution, 'We think that we think.' This is inclined to occur when one of his characters has a set piece of 'thinking' to do, a decision to make, and it is the crisis that reveals the 'thinking' to be not quite so rational a process as we generally understand it to be. When Roger Carbury in *The Way We Live Now* is coming around to his decision to give up Hetta to Paul, Trollope writes:

> After some loose fashion we turn over things in our mind and ultimately reach some decision, guided probably by our feelings at the last moment rather than by any process of ratiocination;—and then we think that we have thought. But to follow out one argument to an end, and then to found on the base so reached the commencement of another, is not common to us (xcɪɪɪ).

Similarly, Doctor Thorne

> walked very slowly . . . thinking over the whole matter; thinking of it, or rather trying to think of it. When a man's heart is warmly concerned in any matter, it is almost useless for him to endeavour to think of it. Instead of thinking, he gives play to his feelings, and feeds his passion by indulging it (*Doctor Thorne*, xɪv).

Or Mary Lawrie in *An Old Man's Love* tries to consider a proposal.

> But, as is so usual with the world at large, she had thought altogether of the past, and not of the future. . . . When we think that we will make our calculations as to the future, it is so easy to revel in our memories instead. Mary had, in truth, not thought of her answer (ɪv).

As human beings go, all these—Roger Carbury, Doctor Thorne, Mary Lawrie—are of the better sort: not at all stupid, and not at all inclined to self-deceit, and all concerned to make the right, the moral, decision; and yet their thought processes do not seem to serve. In the case of Everett Wharton, in *The Prime Minister*, one might expect some self-deceit, for although he is not a bad man, he is not very good, and he is more conceited and officious than most. It is almost embarrassing, then, to have his thought processes denigrated in terms that apply—perhaps—rather widely:

> He had read much, and, though he generally forgot what he read, there were left with him from his readings certain nebulous lights begotten by other men's thinking which enabled him to talk on most subjects. It cannot be said of him that he did much thinking for himself;—but he thought that he thought (II).

We have a different sort of man in Frank Houston, in *Ayala's Angel*. Frank might be expected to know the worst of himself and of mankind; he is sceptical, articulate, witty, cynical. He sets aside three days·at his club to make his decision: whether to persist in the pursuit of the cloddish Gertrude Tringle and her money, or to marry the penniless but charming Imogene Docimer. Trollope comments:

> It may be a question whether three days are ever much better than three minutes for such a purpose. A man's mind will very generally refuse to make itself up until it be driven and compelled by emergency. The three days are passed not in forming but in postponing judgement. In nothing is procrastination so tempting as in thought. So it came to pass, that through the Thursday, the Friday and the Saturday, Frank Houston came to no conclusion, though he believed that every hour of the time was devoted to forming one (XLI).

Circumstances mercifully relieve him: there is a quarrel at the club and a great question over whether a certain member's behaviour requires expulsion, and this question demands a great deal of serious discussion among all the members on hand. What actually 'drives and compels' Frank to his decision is the fortuitous arrival of a letter from Gertrude, which reminds him with a terrible emphasis of her gracelessness, and suddenly the witty Imogene is irresistible.[24]

These frequent deflations of 'thought' and 'reason' in the novels are not mere scintillations of a sceptical wit: they come out of Trollope's view that human behaviour tends to the irrational or absurd. This is why, I think, there is among his characters a striking collection of finely realised people who are extreme types of the irrational. He interests himself in these cases just because they are so extremely 'human,' in this sense. Like later psychologists, he is able to say a great deal about normalcy by his studies of the abnormal. They are all people who seem 'driven,' daemonic or possessed, even. Lord Chiltern (of *Phineas Finn* and *Phineas Redux*) is one: he is just urbane enough to be admitted into drawing-room comedy, but has nevertheless something of a terrible force about him that is particularly recalcitrant to reason, a threat of cruelty. Although he is sure Violet is the one person who can save him, he goes about the winning of her in a contrary way, a way recognisably the least likely to win her. Violet knows the worst of him, and finally accepts him. We do not see much of the marriage, and no doubt Violet was able to soften some of his harshness. When we do glimpse them long after, Lord Chiltern has presumably found himself as a dedicated Master of the Fox Hounds, and Violet still has her verve, and shares a *mot* and a laugh with Lady Glencora (*American Senator*, XXXVI and XXXVII). But it is an effect of the vivid realisation of Chiltern's character that the reader feels for Violet in that marriage and knows there have been difficulties of a severe sort. Vavasor in *Can You Forgive Her?* also exemplifies this terrible unreasonable force, and in his case it does indeed erupt into physical cruelty. Laura Kennedy's husband, in *Phineas Finn* and *Phineas Redux*, is another variation; in him we see an irrational jealousy becoming psychopathic. In *Lady Anna* the obsessive is, this time, a woman. With the Countess, Anna's mother, an abstract principle has become an *idée fixe*, to the point of an attempted murder, and we see the predilection as in all these characters to torture those they love. In Louis Trevelyan, in

He Knew He Was Right, the most detailed study Trollope makes of the obsessive, we see a mind driving itself past the point of sanity, and that point is considered with precision and insight and the most astonishing sympathy. We are led to consider how the moral perspective changes when that point—so hard to determine—is past. When it is past, we know with Emily his wife that the most humane thing she can do is to lie to him, falsely confessing that adultery which of all things he wants assurance of, obsessively seeking out his own destruction.

This contrariety of man is one of Trollope's recurrent themes. At times he will take it up lovingly, as mere frailty: 'The parish parson,' he writes in *The Clergymen of the Church of England*, 'generally has a grievance and is much attached to it—in which he is like all other men in all other walks of life.'[25] In the case of Louis Trevelyan, he takes up the contrariety in its purest because most extreme form, where the unreason, present in all men to some extent, becomes a force of self-destruction. There can be no doubt as to the general significance Trollope attaches to the study of Trevelyan's case; at one stage he observes: 'They who do not understand that a man may be brought to hope that which of all things is the most grievous to him, have not observed with sufficient closeness the perversity of the human mind' (XXXVIII).

Josiah Crawley, in *The Last Chronicle of Barset*, who is probably his most brilliant achievement in a single character, is also, I think, his most careful study of human perversity. He is not mad, like Trevelyan, but feels himself threatened with madness, and is frequently referred to as 'half-mad.' Trollope places him in circumstances that push his endurance very near the breaking point. Although a spiritually dedicated man, Crawley suffers acutely from poverty: as he himself says to his poor parishioners, 'Poverty makes the spirit poor, and the hands weak, and the heart sore—and too often makes the conscience dull' (LXIX). It is painful for him to receive charity from his peer, and so he would indeed be liable to forget just where or how the cheque he is accused of having appropriated did come from. One might call it Freudian forgetting. But anyway he is so dedicated in his vocation that he is inclined to slight temporal matters for spiritual. Elijah does not keep accounts with the ravens. All this is not perversity in itself, but it all puts him in circumstances that force his perversity. We find him, in all his wonderfully indicated complexity, to have a gift for suffering; he courts destruction, he persistently denies his own best good, denies help, denies the support of the kind Robarts. He is forever atoning for a very problematical crime, even in those small things which surprise us into amusement: at the hotel on his way to London, 'They did their best to make him comfortable, and, I think, almost disappointed him in not heaping further misfortunes on his head' (XXXII). In a chapter where Trollope describes him in his very nadir (XLI)—and surely it is one of the most acute pieces of psychological description of the century—he is somehow able to relate Crawley's extreme irrationality to our own ordinary human-ness. We find him contemplating suicide, and then even for a fleeting instant, the murder of his wife and children, for 'only that was wanting to make him of all men the most unfortunate.' Still more remarkable, this man himself knows his own perversity, sees himself revelling in his suffering, dramatising it in that pompous way of his. He seeks to see himself as 'of all men, the most unfortunate,' because he has a propensity to be the scapegoat of humanity. When his friend Arabin tells him of the Holy Land, and how the exact location of the crucifixion is uncertain, Crawley says *he* would know, *he* would know and recognise the actual place of Calvary! (LXXIX)

In this same novel we re-encounter Archdeacon Grantly who is himself a fine study in another kind of perversity. When Trollope observes—as Grantly has been losing an argument to his wife—that Grantly 'was apt at such moments to think that she took an unfair advantage of him by keeping her temper' (LVI), the observation is funny, really just because it is a brilliant discovery of a psychological truth. *À propos* of the Grantlys again, he demonstrates the more ordinary contrariness of a family quarrel. 'It would be wrong to say that love produces quarrels; *but . . .*' and he goes on to anatomise this common occurrence, showing how we 'nurse our wrath lest it cool,' against someone we love best of all, and are supremely wretched in doing so, and yet the beloved one is never more beloved than then! (XLIX). In a more general comment, he declares 'the cross-grainedness of men is so great that things will often be forced to go wrong, even when they have the strongest possible natural tendency of their own to go right' (LVIII).

There is an interesting irony even in the fact that Crawley, this most 'gross-grained' of men, is also one of the most brilliant of men, the most learned, not only in literature and theology but also in that 'true philosophy' of morals. We know him as the peer or superior of the distinguished Dean Arabin; he dowers his otherwise portionless daughters with the knowledge of Greek drama, and his own self-knowledge is almost unbearably acute. Yet it would seem that in this case the brilliance has functioned to find out new turns in contrariety, new discoveries of moral paradox, new virtuosity in the appreciation of ethical dilemmas. Crawley denies 'common' sense, the easy-going practical ethics of such men as Robarts, and of such 'sensible' people as his wife. The more agile the mind, the more ingenious to find new ways of un-reason.

Even Trollope's interest in suicide is part of his interest in man's cross-grainedness—it is surprisingly frequent in his work. In this very novel, there is one actual suicide, that of Dobbs-Broughton, and suicide is considered by Crawley, by the Bishop, by Crosbie—a rather high frequency for a good-humoured Victorian novel. Other closely observed suicides occur in *The Bertrams, The Way We Live Now, The Prime Minister, The Spotted Dog.* Man seeks his own destruction in many ways, and Trollope is always deflating his claim to rationality. The greatest happiness of the greatest number, indeed!

From a writer with so vivid a sense of man's irrationality, we can hardly expect much importance to be attached to man's 'beliefs.' He might rather be expected to say with Keats: 'I have never yet been able to perceive how anything can be known for truth by consecutive reasoning.' We remember his bold statement in the *Cicero* as to how the human intellect has not even been able to establish 'a theory of truth.' Accordingly one deliberately equivocates on doctrine. But in those trenchant sketches on *The Clergyman of the Church of England*, although we find his novelistic bent at work, and his types try to turn into individuals whose story we should like to know, he does nevertheless commit himself to literal, not dramatic, statements on doctrinal matters rather more than he does in the novels or even in the *Cicero*. It is in 'The Clergyman Who Subscribes for Colenso' where he is clearest. For instance, in noting changes of thought, he observes how the 'Broad' churchman used to be he who was tolerant of the doubts of others, but now this churchman has himself given up Bible chronology, many of the miracles, and he ventures yet further forward. The 'meek old-world clergyman' dares no longer teach certain literal things now, though he hardly knows why not; for he has been 'leavened unconsciously by the free-thinking of his liberal brother.'[26] And he writes wittily of how the Broad churchman in London is acceptable and effective, but how in the country, among 'antediluvian rectors and pietistic vicars' he is hated. They hate his teaching, and hate his 'absence of esprit de corps.' 'He has taken orders, simply to upset the Church! He believes in nothing!' But then, writes Trollope,

> It is very hard to come at the actual belief of any man. Indeed how should we hope to do so when we find it so very hard to come at our own? How many are there among us who, in this matter of our religion, which of all things is the most important to us, could take pen in hand and write down even

for their own information exactly what they themselves believe? Not very many clergymen even, if so pressed, would insert boldly and plainly the fulminating clause of the Athanasian Creed; and yet each clergyman declares aloud that he believes it a dozen times every year of his life. Most men who call themselves Christians would say that they believed the Bible, not knowing what they meant, never having attempted,—and very wisely having refrained from attempting amidst the multiplicity of their worldly concerns,—to separate historical record from inspired teaching. But when a liberal-minded clergyman does come among us,—come among us, that is, as our pastor,—we feel not unnaturally a desire to know what it is, at any rate, that he disbelieves. On what is he unsound, according to the orthodoxy of our old friend the neighbouring rector? And are we prepared to be unsound with him? We know that there are some things which we do not like in the teaching to which we have been hitherto subjected;—that fulminating clause, for instance, which tells us that nobody can be saved unless he believes a great deal which we find it impossible to understand; the ceremonial Sabbath which we know that we do not observe, though we go on professing that its observance is a thing necessary for us,—the incompatibility of the teaching of Old Testament records with the new teachings of the rocks and stones. Is it within our power to get over our difficulties by squaring our belief with that of this new parson whom we acknowledge at any rate to be a clever fellow? Before we can do so we must at any rate know what is the belief,—or the unbelief,—that he has in him.

But this is exactly what we never can do. The old rector was ready enough with his belief. There were the three creeds, and the thirty-nine articles; and, above all, there was the Bible,—to be taken entire, unmutilated, and unquestioned. His task was easy enough, and he believed that he believed what he said that he believed. But the new parson has by no means so glib an answer ready to such a question. He is not ready with his answer because he is ever thinking of it. The other man was ready because he did not think. Our new friend, however, is debonair and pleasant to us, with something of a subrisive smile in which we rather feel than know that there is a touch of irony latent. The question asked troubles him inwardly, but he is well aware that he should show no outward trouble. So he is debonair and kind,

—still with that subrisive smile,—and bids us say our prayers, and love our God, and trust our Saviour. The advice is good, but still we want to know whether we are to pray God to help us to keep the Fourth Commandment, or only pretend so to pray,—and whether, when the fulminating clause is used, we are to try to believe it or to disbelieve it. We can only observe our new rector, and find out from his words and his acts how his own mind works on these subjects.

It is soon manifest to us that he has accepted the teaching of the rocks and stones, and that we may give up the actual six days, and give up also the deluge as a drowning of all the world. Indeed, we had almost come to fancy that even the old rector had become hazy on these points. And gradually there leak out to us, as to the falling of manna from heaven, and as to the position of Jonah within the whale, and as to the speaking of Balaam's ass, certain doubts, not expressed indeed, but which are made manifest to us as existing by the absence of expressions of belief. In the intercourse of social life we see something of a smile cross our new friend's face when the thirty-nine articles are brought down beneath his nose. Then he has read the *Essays and Reviews*, and will not declare his opinion that the writers of them should be unfrocked and sent away into chaos;—nay, we find that he is on terms of personal intimacy with one at least among the number of those writers. And, lastly, there comes out a subscription list for Bishop Colenso, and we find our new rector's name down for a five-pound note! That we regard as the sign, to be recognised by us as the most certain of all signs, that he has cut the rope which bound his barque to the old shore, and that he is going out to sea in quest of a better land. Shall we go with him, or shall we stay where we are?

If one could stay, if one could only have a choice in the matter, if one could really believe that the old shore is best, who would leave it? Who would not wish to be secure if he knew where security lay? But this new teacher, who has come among us with his ill-defined doctrines and his subrisive smile,—he and they who have taught him,—have made it impossible for us to stay.[27]

It is clear to Trollope that we must face up to a new relativism. If one could stay with the old absolutes, the old faith, one would. But the new teachings 'have made it impossible for us to stay.' One catches the Victorian note of nostalgia for the old faith, but it is only a note. Trollope does not dwell on it. Since he is sceptical as to whether doctrine ever matters much, he is not much stricken to realise that one kind of doctrine is now invalidated.

Religion, with him, is not a matter of abstract truth; it is, rather, a fact of the human psyche. It is as though he is anticipating William James: Religion is, he implies with a phrase in *Marion Fay*, 'a tone of mind' (xvi). In *Marion Fay*, the charming young Lord Hampstead, an agnostic who has fallen in love with a devout Quaker-cum-Anglican girl, asserts, tolerantly,

> With all my self-assurance I never dare to tamper with the religious opinions of those who are younger or weaker than myself. I feel that they at any rate are safe if they are in earnest. No-one, I think, has ever been put in danger by believing Christ to be God.

(Huxley and Spencer and Butler are hardly so tolerant as this!) 'They none of them know what they believe,' counters Hampstead's friend Roden, who may seem a little familiar, being a thoughtful young Post Office clerk, a man with a ready 'laugh in his eye.' 'Nor do you or I. Men talk of belief as though it were a settled thing. It is so but with few; and that only with those who lack imagination' (xvi). This statement takes us farther in relativism: not only are beliefs generally indefinable, but to have settled beliefs is the mark of 'those who lack imagination,' those, surely, of limited mind. It is fruitless, or foolish, then, to concern ourselves much with these abstractions called 'beliefs.' In *The Way We Live Now*, there is a significant contrast between two friends of Roger Carbury, one an Anglican Bishop, the other a Roman Catholic priest (xv, xvi, lxxxvii). The priest is honest and good, and so zealous, so devoted to his doctrine, that he must proselytise, and social intercourse with him becomes impossible. The other friend, the Bishop, is likewise honest and good, and thoroughly loved throughout his diocese. His

sermons are short and full of much ethical wisdom. The nature
of his beliefs, no one knows! If he had 'doubts,' we are told,
he kept them to himself (xvi). 'Truth' matters very little,
or a 'theory of truth,' or 'belief,' Trollope would say. What
does matter is our own empirical sense of goodness, of truth-
fulness, of honour in social intercourse, of *honestum*, of
humanitas. What we can know, is something of man's nature.
And religion, or the institution that fosters a religious 'tone
of mind'—not any abstract 'truth'—has seemed to serve
this nature well. So, then, Trollope's religion is psyche-centred.
So it is that he can write with amusing tenderness of those two
gentle spinsters, Miss Baker and Miss Mackenzie: 'They both
wished to be religious, having *strong faith in the need for the
comfort of religion* [italics mine]' (*Miss Mackenzie*, ix). And
when in the *Clergymen of the Church of England* he regrets the
passing of much of the old ceremoniousness enveloping the
Archbishops, he writes: 'To be able to venerate is a high
quality, and it is coming to that with us, that we do not now
venerate much.'[28] The orientation is clear: the value of the
spinsters' 'faith' is emphatically empiric, and the value of
Archbishops consists in the value of veneration to the
venerators.

Religion then, is certainly, by and large, a beneficent force.
He applauds Cicero when Cicero insists on the public usefulness of religious observance. Cicero holds that 'it might be the
duty of the state to foster observances, and even to punish
their non-observance—for the benefit of the whole—even
though [the truths assumed] might not in themselves be
true.'[29] Cicero, says Trollope,

> repudiates the belief [in augury, etc.] as unreasonable or
> childish, but recommends that men should live as though
> they believed. In such a theory as this, put thus before the
> reader, there will seem to be dissimulation. I cannot deny
> that it is so, though most anxious to assert the honesty of
> Cicero. I can only say that such dissimulation did prevail then,
> and that it does prevail now. If any be great enough to con-

demn the hierarchs of all the churches, he may do so, and
may include Cicero with the Archbishop of Canterbury. I am
not. It seems unnecessary to make allowances for the advanc-
ing intelligence of men, and unwise to place yourself so far
ahead as to shut yourself out from that common pale of mankind. I distrust the self-confidence of him who thinks that he
can deduce from one acknowledged error a whole scheme of
falsehood.[30]

And he quotes Cicero:

Former ages erred in much which we know to have been
changed by practice, by doctrine, or by time. But the custom,
the religion, the discipline, the laws of the augurs and the
authority of the college, are retained, in obedience to the
opinion of the people, and to the great good of the State.[31]

Then Trollope adds:

No stronger motive for adhering to religious observances can
be put forward than the opinion of the people and the good
of the State. There will be they who aver that truth is great
and should be allowed to prevail. Though broken worlds
should fall in disorder round their heads, they would stand
firm amid the ruins. But they who are likely to be made
responsible will not cause worlds to be broken.[32]

The strength of society seems to be in its institutions; it
exists through and in custom and convention.

So we see Trollope arrived at much the same position as the
'thinkers,' like George Eliot, or like Arnold. George Eliot
especially is in many ways particularly close to Trollope. She
will often take up cases of moral paradox in terms basically
like Trollope's, even so specifically as the 'worldly' clergyman
like Mr. Irwine being demonstrably more useful and more
charitable than the reforming evangelical Mr. Roe who pro-
fesses to be morally superior. Mr. Irwine

thought the custom of baptism more important than its
doctrine, and that the religious benefits . . . were but slightly
dependent on a clear understanding of the Liturgy or the
sermon (*Adam Bede*, vi).

111

She has, like Trollope, 'an occasional tenderness for old abuses . . . and a sigh for the departed shades of vulgar errors' (*Amos Barton*, i). Her ironic sense of the incongruities of life are very strong, too; and she too is a declared relativist and casuist. In *Middlemarch*, when Casaubon seems unquestionably malignant, she warns us against judging: 'I protest,' she says, 'against any absolute conclusion' (x), and she exacts our pity for the man as he is forced to recognise his own triviality. George Eliot's own household philosopher, the brilliant George Henry Lewes, is himself known for his philosophical and critical relativism. But Trollope is the best relativist as novelist. He is able to see 'belief' as something much less portentous than his earnest contemporaries saw it. The heady excitement of George Eliot's discovery of The Higher Criticism was not for him. Nor was Tennyson's sickening sense of loss. Nor was Arnold's desolation. He was never, like Arnold, caught in that enervating process, 'the dialogue of the mind with itself.' Although he does feel Arnold's nostalgia for the old religion, he does not linger in it; but rather frees himself of the pain by ironic self-mockery. He sees in himself the taste for 'the sweet medieval flavour of old English corruption.'[33]

George Eliot, even though she comes round to veneration for custom and established religion, always bears the marks of her rebellion against literal religion. She is unwilling to take up the hypocrisy that Trollope feels is for the public good, and she is not *enough* of a relativist to be at ease in a conventional church. Her admirable but awkward honesty is instanced in a letter to Trollope himself. Trollope has just written her a letter of praise and thanks for *Felix Holt*, and has been kind beyond the line of ordinary friendship in sharing with Lewes his specially imported Cuban cigars. She is touched by the letter, and loves Trollope anyway, 'one of the heartiest, most genuine, moral and generous men we know.'[34] She writes in reply to Trollope:

> All goodness in the world bless you! First, for being what you are. Next for the regard I think you bear toward that (to

me) best of men, my dear husband. And after those two chief things, for the goodness and sympathy you have long shown both in word and act towards me in particular. That is the answer I at once made inwardly on reading your letter so I wrote it down without addition.[35]

It is a charming letter, and possibly, as she says, written, on the impulse of the moment. And yet is there not a very peculiar unidiomatic opening, for an impulsive utterance? Is there not, in fact, a considered revision in this awkward periphrasis to avoid the word God, just because she feels it would be dishonest in her to use the word? Trollope is never troubled by such scruples: whatever God is, He is at the very least an indispensable linguistic convenience.

We have seen Trollope grant, with Cicero, that even 'dishonest' religious observances are for the public good. And in his tender portrait of 'The Parson of the Parish,' another of the sketches of the *Clergymen,* he condones the Parson's degree of hypocrisy.

Against gross profligacy and loud sin he can inveigh boldly ... but with the peccadilloes dear to the rustic mind he knows how to make compromises, and can put up with a little drunkenness, with occasional sabbath-breaking, with ordinary oaths, and with church somnolence. He does not expect much of poor human nature, and is thankful for moderate results. ... He loves his religion and wages an honest fight with the devil; but even with the devil he likes to deal courteously, and is not averse to some occasional truces. . . . *It almost seems that something approaching to hypocrisy were a necessary component part of the character of the English parish parson, and yet he is a man always alert to be honest* [italics mine]. . . . He cannot tell his people what amount of religion will really suffice for them, knowing that he will never get from them all that he asks; and thus he is compelled to have an inner life and an outer,—an inner life, in which he squares his religious views with his real ideas as to that which God requires from his creatures; and an outer life, in which he is always demanding much in order that he may get little.[36]

Trollope understands the function of the Anglican church as

adapting itself to the expediency of the situation. Like Cicero's good man in politics, it will shake hands with evil in order to effect the greater good. It had better 'not expect much of poor human nature,' for it is human to 'know the better course and take the worse,' and to continually refuse to make use of 'the wisdom which is at our fingers' ends.' Poor Josiah Crawley, knowing the unreason of man and his own nightmare threat of madness, shows his own moral insight on the occasion of Mrs. Proudie's death:

> No doubt the finite and meagre nature of our feelings does prevent us from extending our sympathies to those whom we have not seen in the flesh. It should not be so, and would not with one who had nurtured his heart with proper care. . . . But do not suppose, sir, that I complain of this man or that woman because his sympathies, or hers, run out of that course which my reason tells me they should hold. The man with whom it would not be so would simply be a god among men. It is in his perfection as a man that we recognise the divinity of Christ. It is in the imperfection of men that we recognise our necessity for a Christ (*Last Chronicle*, LXVIII).

Here is a pretty twist given to Christian paradox! There is nothing here, it must be emphasised, of orthodox Christian supernaturalism. Of course it is not Trollope who speaks, it is Josiah Crawley; but Crawley could not say this if Trollope hadn't thought of it. Trollope grants that we have advantages in moral perception since Christ; but I think he really sees this advantage as having been the achievement of the idea of Christ, not at all the fact of an historical Christ and a crucifixion. The idea of Christ is only a recognition of man's irrationality; and the sense of original sin is only an admission of man's perversity.

Trollope's Anglicanism, then, has nothing of supernaturalism except paradoxically: the 'divine' is the idea of the perfection of the human. Yet one cannot say Trollope is a materialist any more than one can say it of Carlyle. If Carlyle proclaims a 'natural supernaturalism' in such wonders as the daily sunrise, Trollope finds his wonders in the variety and contrariety and the concept of goodness displayed by the human mind. 'The natural goodness of some men is a problem which we cannot solve.'[37] His own religious 'tone of mind' shows itself in the careful consideration of and concern for human beings, in taking each individual character in each individual case as marvellous in its individuation, and as worthy of special consideration.

*   *   *

Readers who come new to Trollope, starting as most do with the Barchester series, are generally quite struck to find someone writing so extensively and knowingly about ecclesiastical matters without writing about religion. We assume that conventional Victorians—and Trollope is obviously conventional—could hardly concern themselves so much with the Church without some sort of declared piety. I hope it may now appear that it is his antidogmatic position that enables him to achieve his ironic perspective, and to exploit his ironic situation. Only by such detachment can the novelist turn a subject so controversial as ecclesiastical reform into a substantial non-controversial novel, as he does in *The Warden* and in *Barchester Towers*.

Some others of his novels demonstrate how 'less certainty' gives the novelist 'more scope.' *The Bertrams* is one such, and is particularly noteworthy in that the novel as a whole deflates rationality in religion. George Bertram is a young man of distinguished intellect and academic training, resolved to devote himself to the service of God and mankind as a minister of the Church. While he is on tour in the Holy Land—or on a pilgrimage, rather—he is taken up by a pleasant social circle whose leader is the very sociable Miss Todd, a great organiser of picnics. Now, although it was apparently a rather fashionable thing to visit the Holy Land, and no doubt there were many pleasant meetings among the English there,[38] Trollope nevertheless makes capital out of the incongruity of a jolly outing in the actual places of Christ's ministry, 'a large party immediately over the ashes of James the Just' (IX). In the middle of this incongruity, Bertram falls in love with Caroline Waddingham, an attractive girl with a little gift for witty mockery. He confides to her his vocation, and she makes pleasant fun of it. 'He had not strength of character to laugh at her description and yet to be unmoved by it. He must either resent what she said, or laugh and be ruled by it' (X). So simply, but with such exquisite precision Trollope presents a very subtle psychological state. These few words epitomise the man's character and the moral problem. Trollope has made Caroline's conversation really amusing, so that we must laugh with Bertram. And he has made us familiar with the degree of pride in Bertram's character, a pride that is so slight and so common a failing there would be few readers who could not feel with him, and yet it is this degree of pride that makes him vulnerable. In this moment of light conversation Bertram's life is changed; his vow is made null by the laughter of this girl. He becomes engaged to her, and because with his lively intellect and learning he must be *something*, he turns from orthodoxy to the Higher Criticism, and becomes a 'rationalist.' When Caroline puts off the wedding, he writes a shocking book along the lines of Feuerbach and Strauss. When she breaks the engagement, he writes another. So trivial the forces may be, Trollope implies, that affect men's 'beliefs.' Trollope deflates even his love; if Bertram had been seeing Caroline more often, 'it is probable enough that he might by this time have been half tired of her' (XIII). But he continues to be victimised by the love. His loss of religious faith would seem to matter very little, but his moral delinquency matters. His sense of his own worth as a man is an admirable thing, and yet it makes him vulnerable to the hurt of idle ridicule. Both Caroline and Bertram run their course of life with a sort of moral shabbiness for which rationalism, or a sense of one's own worth, or principles of simplistic 'honesty,' are not sufficient antidote.

Julius Mackenzie, in the short story 'The Spotted Dog,' is another apostate, who, though briefly drawn, nevertheless catches some light of the tragic. Mackenzie is actuated by principles of honesty and republicanism: he forsakes the Church because his intellect rejects the doctrine of the Trinity, and he marries a prostitute because he wants to 'save' her. His principles trap him into a chain of rather Zola-esque horror: alcoholism, a betrayal of the ideal of scholarship which alone was holy to him, and finally, suicide. It is another instance of the ironic juxtaposition of *Fiat justitia* and *rem si possis recte*. Take cruel honesty, or take kindly hypocrisy.

By and large Trollope certainly holds that the influence of Christianity is benign. And yet, just because he does so, he interests himself in those cases where this good thing, religion, results in evil: *Tantum religio potuit suadore malorum.* Iphigenia is more than once laid on the altar of a cruel religion. In *John Caldigate*, Trollope exacts some sympathy for pietistic Mrs. Bolton in the practice of her religion, but the practice includes cruelty. The terrible night of the meeting of wills, Clara's and her mother's, is an appallingly successful study in domestic sadism. This situation is subsidiary in *John Caldigate*, but a similar one is central in *Linda Tressel*. In both cases, religion has become obsessive. Both parallel another case of maternal obsession, that of the Countess in *Lady Anna*, where the *idée fixe* is not religious but social. But all three cases exemplify an abstract principle perverting parental love into outrageous cruelty.

It is true that when religion is obsessive in Trollope's novels, the religion is an evangelical one. He would claim for the old High Anglicanism that in its non-enthusiasm it is unlikely to become obsessive. It is one of his favourite ironies that the easygoing High Church clergyman is more charitable, in fact, or in cases, and exercises more of the Christian virtues than the reforming evangelicals, who make the greater claim to them. As a general rule, throughout the novels, we do not like the evangelicals, from Slope on. But we cannot say that

Trollope is doctrinaire even here. There is a shadow of a shadow of sympathy for Slope, in the end of *Barchester Towers*, and there is the substance of sympathy for Mrs. Proudie before her death in *The Last Chronicle*. Trollope weighs up the good and evil of her, and concludes that although undoubtedly she effected more evil than good, her motives were nevertheless more good than evil. After Slope, evangelical clergymen are less caricatured, and more kindly treated. Puddleham in *The Vicar of Bullhampton* is not very bright, but he is not very vicious. Maguire and Stumfold in *Miss Mackenzie* are mixed. The scheme of this last novel puts a new realistic turn to the *Everyman* theme. Miss Mackenzie is Everywoman, and Low and High Church struggle to win her soul. But Low and High Church come in the form of human ministers, and it seems that they are really concerned to win her allegiance and her money, not her soul. And then her soul at the end seems to find its own best salvation in a marriage to a widower who needs her help, her money, and her gentle loving self all at the same time. The actual issue deflates the importance of the doctrinal issues.

A most interesting evangelical clergyman turns up in *The Claverings*. In this novel, the Reverend Harry Clavering has a curate, Mr. Saul, who seems at first to be in a class with Mr. Slope. Saul surprises us by falling genuinely in love with Clavering's pretty and charming daughter Fanny, and Fanny surprises everybody by falling genuinely in love with Saul. Clavering is one of those attractive hunting parsons: 'he was a kind, soft-hearted, gracious man . . . and awake—though not widely awake—to the responsibilities of his calling. The world had been too comfortable for him, and also too narrow; so that he had sunk into idleness' (11). Saul, though less attractive, is honestly zealous, and Fanny Clavering, even before her interest in Saul, is actually more devoted to her own sphere of work in the parish schools than her father is to his. It is truly a common piety that brings Saul and Fanny together. Then the father must face his own moral problem.

He tolerates zeal in his curate, but it horrifies him in a suitor for his daughter. While we grow to admire Saul's devotion and integrity, Clavering grows to realise how he himself has defected from a Christian ideal. Good man that he is, he is made painfully aware of how he has no real case whatsoever against the marriage. Saul exemplifies better than he does himself those virtues he himself stands for. So he must resign his daughter to Saul cheerfully, and the circumstances also exact that he resign the living to him. He is not without regret, however; he ruefully sees how it will be: 'There are to be no more cakes and ale in the parish' (XLVIII). The story of this courtship demonstrates once more the Trollopian ambiguity of situation: the Puritan way can have its moral beauties too.

But, as everybody knows, for the most part Trollope's High Churchman comes out ahead. When he makes his most exacting test of charity, he gives us his most charitable parson to deal with it, and the parson is a type of the old-fashioned High Churchman, graceful and urbane and casuistical. The exacting test is the case of Carry Brattle, the 'fallen woman' in *The Vicar of Bullhampton*, and the vicar is the engaging Frank Fenwick. The contrast between Fenwick's charity, and the dissenting Puddleham's failure in charity is made very clear, partly by means of a comic conflict over the site of the new Puddlehamite chapel. There are fine ploys made, and counterploys and outploys, with Frank Fenwick generally hoisting Puddleham on his own petard. Before Fenwick's advent, Puddleham

> had always previously enjoyed the privilege of being on bad terms with the clergymen of the Establishment. It had been his glory to be a poacher on another man's manor, to filch souls, as it were . . . and to obtain recognition of his position by the activity of his operations in the guise of a blister. Our Vicar, understanding something of this, had, with some malice towards the gentleman himself, determined to rob Mr. Puddleham of his blistering powers. . . . [Puddleham] was painfully conscious of the guile of this young man, who had,

as it were, cheated him out of that appropriate acerbity of religion, without which a proselyting sect can hardly maintain its ground beneath the shadow of an endowed and domineering Church (xxxv).

Frank, like many of Trollope's most delightful people, is himself a witty ironist. Though he loathes the prospect of the new chapel being built in sight of his own house, and loathes it (like the dissenter's religion) for its *ugliness*, he refuses to admit its offensiveness, and annoys his family by a hypocritical cheerfulness about it. To his dear friend Gilmore he does confess his loathing, however, and playfully, the use of its ugliness. 'It shall be my hair shirt, my fast . . . my little pet good work. . . . There is not a dissenter in Bullhampton will get so much out of the chapel as I will' (lvi). And he is able generally to keep the advantage. But although in the end the chapel goes, Frank himself is outwitted. The Marquis, who by Puddleham's machinations had involved himself in the conflict, and had certainly offended Frank by complaining of him to his Bishop, just as certainly now owes Frank an apology. But the Marquis has a son who has ten times the brain of his father, and who is able to one-up' Fenwick, asking him for peace 'for the sake of Christian charity and goodwill,' beating him on his own ground, as Fenwick has beaten Puddleham. Fenwick had been looking forward to the Marquis's apology so that he might indulge in the pleasure of graciously forgiving him. 'He felt he was being cunningly cheated out of his grievance' (lxx). But of course he must give in.

All this one-upping about the chapel forms a light counterpoint to the conflict over the case of Carry Brattle. Here Fenwick takes on not only Puddleham, but the whole of *unco guid* society. Again and again he, and then Trollope, insist on how disproportionate is society's punishment, for 'so small a crime' (xxvii, xxxix, liii). Carry has been seduced, and now society makes it almost impossible for her to do anything but compound the crime and turn to prostitution. 'If we left the doors of our prisons open, and then expressed disgust because the prisoners walked out, we should hardly be less rational' (LII). Frank searches for a way to bring Carry back into decency, and goes so far as to promise her a home. Even Frank's good wife Janet thinks this will be too difficult.

> 'But how is it possible, Frank?' [she asks,] 'Where can you find a home for her?'
> 'She has a married sister, Janet,' [says Frank.]
> 'Who would not speak to her, or let her inside the door of her house! Surely, Frank, you know the unforgiving nature of women of that class for such sin as poor Carry Brattle's?'
> 'I wonder whether they ever say their prayers.'
> 'Of course they do. Mrs. Gay, no doubt, is a very religious woman. But it is permitted to them not to forgive that sin.'
> 'By what law?'
> 'By the law of custom' (XXXIX).

Note here, although the conversation is thoroughly, brilliantly, characteristic of Fenwick, he, or Trollope, is playing the naïve *eiron*. The question strikes to the base of the popular Victorian morality. 'The law of custom' is all you can boil this down to. There is no such law inherent in man's nature, and it has nothing to do with Christianity.

Frank has on his side Janet, naturally, and Carry's mother, who will take her in and forgive her. This mother, a humble miller's wife, Trollope takes pains to say, is a 'lady,' for her charity (VII). And the unmarried sister Fanny is forgiving. Against Frank, there is society in general, such as the married sister Mrs. Gay; and then he has against him Carry's father too, Old Brattle, who never goes to church. He is a pagan, we are told, and yet the 'law of custom,' and the father's sense of outrage at the despoiling of the daughter, are too strong in him to permit him to forgive, for a long time. The trial near the end of the book, when Carry's father at last gives her his support when she must stand as a witness in a public law court, is a dramatic occasion that focuses a strong cold light on the inhumanity of society to such as Carry. Frank even has to do battle with Puddleham for Carry's sake. Puddleham has mentioned to the Marquis in Fenwick's presence that the miller's daughter is a—prostitute. And Frank takes him up on it later.

'You don't know it as a fact,' he says.
'Everybody says so.'
'How do you know she has not married, and become an honest woman?'
'It is possible, of course. Though as for that,—when a young woman has once gone astray—'
'As did Mary Magdalene, for instance!'
'Mr. Fenwick, it was a very bad case.'
'And isn't my case very bad, and yours? Are we not in a bad way? Have we not all sinned as to deserve eternal punishment?'
'Certainly, Mr. Fenwick.'
'Then there can't be much difference between her and us. She can't deserve more than eternal punishment' (XVII).

With irreproachable theology, Fenwick gets the advantage of the dissenter. I think thereby Trollope does accomplish something of a 'social purpose,' in fighting a very insidious abuse of the time. But he does not leave it at that. He ranges from a hard-headed display of the psychology of society in a specific matter, far on into concepts of the general nature of man and society. In *An Eye for an Eye*, which also concerns a woman seduced, he emphasises again the strange disproportion in the heavy punishment that falls on the woman, while the man, whose guilt is generally the greater, gets off very lightly. This may come about, he speculates wryly, because 'the world could not afford to ostracise the men—though happily it might condemn the women' (XIX). And in *The Vicar of Bullhampton* he assesses the case in a similarly tough-minded way, but then he also takes it out of its local and timely context into the larger context of the whole human problem of ethics and necessity. Carry's sister Fanny meditates 'on the strange destiny of women'; for in the old days she had sometimes envied this pretty sister with her charming ways. Her own destiny was to be a homely household thing. . . . Fate had made her plain, and no man loved her. The same chance had made Carry pretty, — the belle of the village, the acknowledged beauty of Bullhampton. And there she lay, a thing *said to be* [italics mine] so foul that even a father could not endure to have her name mentioned in his ears. And yet, how small had been her fault compared with other crimes for which men and women are forgiven speedily, even if it has been held that pardon has ever been required (LIII).

The perspective is much larger than the propagandist's. Fanny's speculations here, for instance, put the emphasis on the 'strange destiny of women,' and of men, too, and on the ironies inherent in the human condition. The absurdity of the excessive punishment for this small crime is only one of the absurd ways of mankind. All men and all societies are liable to these absurdities. All we can do, is extend our understanding to each case, and work out an ethical decision with the most *humanitas* available to us, always bending principle to pity.

Trollope's philosophy, his religion, his ethics are really all one: antisystematic, antidoctrinal, antipreceptual. The 'true philosophy' of Cicero is Trollope's Christianity, and his ethics is *humanitas* or charity. Institutions establish the community of men: a 'church' means that many men have had an idea of goodness, but it is part of that goodness to perpetually need to be rediscovered and re-established in the flux of history and of changing, 'reforming' society, in each individual situation. In all this relativism, there is only one anchor, and that is our sense of ourselves and of other people. His realism, and his irony, then, are moral in the widest and deepest sense, and can, perhaps, be called 'religious.'

NOTES

[1]Quoted by André Maurois, as an epigraph to Chapter IX of *Les Silences du Colonel Bramble.*

[2]*Les Mots.* Paris, Gallimard, 1964, p. 80.

[3]London, 1933. Recently W. H. Auden quotes an Anglican Bishop: 'Orthodoxy is Reticence.' *New Yorker*, April 4, 1970, p. 133.

[4]New York, London, Collins; and Farrar, Straus & Cudahy, 1956.

[5]Pp. 89–90.   [6]P. 203.   [7]Pp. 47–48.

[8]Quoted, A. O. J. Cockshut, *Anglican Attitudes*. London, Collins, 1959, p. 63.

[9]'Moral Problems in the Victorian Period,' *Victorian Studies*, IX Supplement, September, 1965, 29–46. This passage, p. 30.

[10]Those modern 'imitations' of Trollope by Ronald Knox and Angela Thirkell, pleasant as they are, only manage to catch some of the Trollopian superficia, missing the essential, which must be a good solid real dilemma, genuinely difficult, whether comic or not.

[11]*Oxford Dictionary of the Christian Church*, London, 1958, under 'Moral Theology.'

[12]Schneewind, note, p. 30.

[13]Schneewind, note, p. 33.

[14]See DNB, article on John Grote.

[15]Lionel Stevenson has blocked out a rich subject in 'The Relativity of Truth in Victorian Fiction,' in *Victorian Essays*, eds. Anderson and Clareson. Ohio, Kent State University Press, 1967, pp. 71–86.

[16]*The Conscience, Lectures on Casuistry*. London, Macmillan, and Cambridge, 1866. p. 131.

[17]P. 21.

[18]Alec R. Vidler, *Witness to the Light*. New York, C. Scribner's Sons, 1948, pp. 9–10; and *F. D. Maurice and Company*. London, S.C.M. Press, 1966, pp. 22–25, *et passim*.

[19]Pp. 163–164.   [20]P. 165 ff.

[21]*Satires*, I, i. 69–70. For Trollope on the moral effectiveness of Horace's method, see *Letters*, p. 266.

[22]*Confessions*, VII, vii, 17.

[23]*Cicero*, II, 325–326.

[24]See also *Warden*, X; *Framley Parsonage*, XXXV; *Sir Harry Hotspur of Humblethwaite*, XX; *Rachel Ray*, XXVIII; *Kept in the Dark* XII; *Castle Richmond*, IX; *Lord Palmerston*, p. 31.

[25]London, Chapman and Hall, 1866, p. 64.

[26]Pp. 119–121.   [27]Pp. 124–128.   [28]Pp. 4–5.

[29]*Cicero*, II, 297.

[30]P. 298.   [31]P. 299.   [32]P. 299.

[33]*Clergymen of the Church of England*. London, Chapman and Hall, 1866, p. 28.

[34]*Letters*, ed. Gordon S. Haight, New Haven, Yale University Press, IV, 59.

[35]P. 296.

[36]Pp. 61–64. See also *Vicar of Bullhampton*, VII.

[37]Trollope's marginal note in Bacon's Essays, 'Of Goodnesse and Goodnesse of Nature.' P. 25, of Michael Sadleir's 'Trollope and Bacon's Essays,' *NCF* [then *The Trollopian*], I, Summer, 1945, 21–34.

[38]Cf. Arabin's trip, in *Last Chronicle*, and *Dr. Thorne*, XXXIII. Cf. also Melville's *Clarel*.

Chapter VI

THE ART OF THE POSSIBLE

Politics are made in time and place. . . .

WALTER BAGEHOT

TROLLOPE'S art, his religion and his philosophy are all demonstrably consistent; and his distinguishing consistency, his 'one-ness,' can best be thought of as a relativism, arrived at by means of the multiple ironic perspective. His 'one-ness,' then, may one say, is really a pluralism. If he had gone in for divinity, he would have qualified as a comparative religionist, both intellectually and emotionally. Or if he had taken up the line of sociological study established by Comte, he would have qualified as a comparative anthropologist. He avers, for instance, when considering the strange courtship customs of the Americans (in the short story 'Miss Ophelia Gledd'), 'these practices are right or wrong, not in accordance with a fixed rule of morality prevailing over all the earth . . . but right or wrong according to the usages of the country in which they are practised.' It is our good fortune that he put this relativism at the service of the art of the novel.

To hold that there can be no absolute basis for morals is not at all to deny or lessen their absolute importance. It would seem, with Trollope, that the admission of relativism makes the study of morals all the more urgent, just as with George Eliot; since 'God' and 'Immortality' are no longer tenable concepts, our moral responsibility is greater, not less. 'Duty! How peremptory and absolute!' In the line of duty, Trollope has such respect for the functional efficacy of conventional religion that he would not willingly stint on his support for it in any way. Therefore he himself as 'weekday preacher' does practice a degree of that benign 'hypocrisy' that he condones in Cicero and in 'The Parson of the Parish.' His own statements on religion, then, stand in need of a little decoding, easy enough when his essential philosophy is clear.

His political views, however, he explains with the utmost clarity. There is no 'hypocrisy' here, only a complicated state of affairs, which he describes perfectly in the *Autobiography* as he recounts his own experiences as unsuccessful candidate for Parliament.[1] He is an 'advanced Conservative–Liberal.' In politics as in religion, he refuses commitment to dogma, to party, to *Fiat justitia*. He can be staunchly loyal to the Anglican Church because it is so blessedly noncommittal; and in politics he is equally loyal to that other entity, the English Constitution, which is, in turn, about as hard to define as the Church. Its origins are hidden in the obscurity of the Anglo-Saxon Witenagemot, or perhaps, as with Miss Thorne's religion, there are still more obscure beginnings in convocations of politic Druids. Its functions are, even now, hidden behind a screen of vestigial forms: the Speech from the Throne, the Woolsack, and the House of Lords. American children think that because England has a Queen it is not a democracy. Like many mistakes of children, this is entirely sensible. England is still, as Walter Bagehot said in Trollope's time, a disguised republic.[2]

We are much in debt to Professor Asa Briggs for demonstrating in his *Victorian People* the great similarity between Trollope and his contemporary, Walter Bagehot, the political economist and man of letters.[3] Briggs collates for us Bagehot's *English Constitution* with Trollope's political writings: there are parallel attitudes, parallel concepts, parallel statements, and then, further, Trollope presents in dramatic form the cases that illustrate Bagehot's themes. Briggs hereby adds to historical understanding, and to political science as well. Criticism is in his debt, too: he suggests new ways of assessing Trollope—the subtle, detached and witty Bagehot has even deeper affinities with Trollope than Briggs has occasion to say. Even as literary critics they are in sympathy; Bagehot's judgments on Thackeray and Dickens are quite in Trollope's vein. But the basic common factor is the ironic turn of mind. What Gertrude Himmelfarb says of Bagehot might be taken to apply to Trollope:

> . . . the peculiar quality of the man and the genius of his work . . . [is] the ability to combine the disparate, to keep in focus at the same time both sides of the moon. . . . If his writings abound in irony and paradox, it is because his sense of reality was multi-faceted.[4]

Bagehot's achievement in *The English Constitution* is itself an ironic juxtaposition of the disparate: on the one hand, the traditional theory of English government, and on the other, the way it actually works. He reveals, for instance, that although everyone has always thought the English Constitution succeeds because its legislative functions are kept separate from its executive, in actuality 'the efficient secret of the English Constitution may be described as the close union, the nearly complete fusion of the executive and legislative powers.'[5] The theory is, and was, so current, he points out, that the framers of the American Constitution, hoping to emulate the success of the English system in this regard, insisted on the separation—whether for better or for worse the literary critic will leave to the political scientist to say. Bagehot thought it was rather for the worse. At any rate, one may see that Bagehot's theme is like Trollope's: the discrepancy between *seems* and *is*, between man's pretensions to rationality and his way of muddling through. He is just as firmly anti-systematic: 'I have for practical purposes no belief in unvarying rules.'[6] He has also Trollope's zest for life, his engagement and sense of moral responsibility (he ran unsuccessfully for Parliament *four* times to Trollope's one). He has, like Trollope, a sense of the mystery of things and of that 'god in man.' 'Bagehot's conviction of man's eternal destiny heightened his sense of the world's absurdity,' writes Norman St. John-Stevas. He quotes Bagehot:

> There seems to be an unalterable contradiction between the human mind and its employments. How can a *soul* be a merchant? What relation to an immortal being have the price of linseed, the fall of butter, the tare on tallow, or the brokerage on hemp? . . . The soul ties its shoe; the mind washes its hands in a basin. All is incongruous.[7]

Such meditations are much in the mode of Trollope, and of his awareness of the double nature of man. It does seem to be this ironic sense of doubleness that leads to detachment, and even specifically to humour. Although Trollope and Bagehot may be the most 'Victorian' of all Victorians—Bagehot has been called 'the greatest Victorian of them all'—there is a refreshingly graceful humour in both that eschews the sometimes oppressive solemnity and the 'terrible earnestness' of such as George Eliot. And the humour does not invalidate the moral points they would make.

For both, as for F. D. Maurice too, the study of political man is of paramount importance. Politics is not a specialised, sharply demarcated field of study; it is only the study of *social* man in his most practical aspects, man trying to act, to achieve something, not by himself, but in concert with other men. We can discover the ways of society through the study of real men functioning in a specific political structure, or government. It is virtually certain, as Briggs says, that Trollope read Bagehot's *English Constitution*; it was running from 1865 to 1867 in *The Fortnightly Review*, which Trollope had helped to found; but we have here not a question of influence in the sense that Bagehot ever changed Trollope's political views. Trollope tells us in his *Autobiography* that they had not changed at all, since he first as a young man began to have them. He has been and is an 'advanced, but still a Conservative–Liberal, which I regard not only as a possible but as a rational and consistent phase of political existence.'[8] And he proceeds to outline that phase, speaking of the pros and cons in both Conservative and Liberal positions, and of how he feels the greatest, safest good is to be attained by compromise. And his studies of politics and elections are not different in orientation between the early *Rachel Ray* (1863) and the post-Bagehot Palliser novels. But we can justifiably imagine he was delighted with Bagehot's work, and that it reinforced his own ideas, and formulated many, so that he was the better able to develop his political studies in the novels, from a more secure foundation. He is especially concerned with politics at the time of these *Fortnightly* essays of Bagehot's: he writes his book on Lord Palmerston in 1867, and he runs for election in Beverley in 1868. Henceforth the political scenes of his novels, though the point of view has not changed, are sharper, more fully drawn, and more searching.

Bagehot's anatomy of the English Constitution objectifies Trollope's assumptions about political life. He says the government consists of two parts, which he calls the *dignified* and the *efficient*. The latter is of course what really gets the work done, while the *dignified* parts in spite of their absurdities have various very important uses. He claims that England's political soundness depends on its being a *deferential* nation. The Queen is something the citizen can understand, and can focus his loyalties and duties on, 'a visible symbol of unity to those still so imperfectly educated as to need a symbol.'[9]

> To state the matter shortly, royalty is a government in which the attention of the nation is concentrated on one person doing interesting actions. A Republic is a government in which attention is divided between many, who are all doing uninteresting actions. Accordingly, so long as the human heart is strong and the human reason weak, royalty will be strong because it appeals to diffused feelings, and Republics weak because they appeal to the understanding.[10]

Like Trollope, Bagehot recognises the contrariness in men's minds undreamt of in utilitarian philosophy.

The *efficient* part of government—Prime Minister, Cabinet, and Commons—has various functions, and these in Bagehot's terms (and Trollope's) are not quite what is traditionally thought. The Commons' *chief* function is not legislative, but elective, Bagehot insists. It does well enough if it chooses and supports a decent executive through a session. It has also an *expressive* function, formulating the feeling of the country on what comes before it. Third, there is what Bagehot calls its *teaching* function; it educates the nation, for there must be parliamentary *debate* and *opposition*: 'The nation is forced to hear two sides—all sides, perhaps.'[11] Fourth, there is the *informing* function; as in medieval times Commons presented grievances to the sovereign, so now it presents them to the nation, and by making the nation aware of injustice, contributes ultimately to the achievement of some sort of justice. Its last function, the *legislative* one, which we tend to think paramount, Bagehot considers less important than the executive function exercised by the Cabinet.

He argues that the English system succeeds as well as any, probably better than any other, in that a deferential people, even if unintelligent, get the best government, for they defer to that class of men best able to govern. That class is 'a select few,' men who have 'a life of leisure, a long culture, a varied experience, an existence by which the judgment is incessantly exercised and by which it may be incessantly improved.'[12] In this way actual stupidity, if deferential, can contribute to the success of a government: this is one of Bagehot's most noteworthy ironies. He is not as arrogantly undemocratic as he may seem; if one considers the period he is anatomising, I think it is clear that he is pretty pragmatic. England being such as it is, in these 1860s, we are obliged to realise that success in government *does* in large measure depend on deference in the lower classes. We do not in America have Bagehot's predilections, and yet he is not altogether irrelevant to any political situation.

Bagehot is, like Trollope, neither Conservative nor Liberal, but in between. Yet where Trollope leans somewhat to the left of centre, Bagehot leans to the right. Trollope has much more of a sense of the movement towards democracy than Bagehot. Briggs, surely, errs a little in emphasis on their common mid-Victorian complacency. Bagehot is more complacent than Trollope, and more distressed by the effects of the second Reform Bill. Countless times in the novels, Trollope states clearly how the country is moving towards democracy; he accepts the fact more boldly than Bagehot, and has more sympathy for liberals. The sympathy is perfectly evident in his portrayal of characters like Ontario Moggs in *Ralph the Heir*, Daniel Thwaite in *Lady Anna*, and various other men of the people. And it is stated best perhaps in his *North America*. Trollope is frank to admit that he, as one of his class, enjoys deference from lower classes; but he appreciates how the American as he loses this deference, the pulling of the forelock, gains in 'manly dignity.'[13] He ends his *North America* with a rather moving tribute to the success of the Great Experiment:

> I claim no credit for the new country. I impute no blame to the old country. But there is the fact. The Irishman when he expatriates himself to one of those American States loses much of affectionate, confiding, master-worshipping nature which makes him so good a fellow when at home. But he becomes more of a man. He assumes a dignity which he never has known before. . . . To me personally he has perhaps become less pleasant than he was. But to himself—! . . . When we speak of America and of her institutions we should remember that she has given to our increasing population rights and privileges which we could not give;—which as an old country we probably can never give. That self-asserting, obtrusive independence which so often wounds us, is, if viewed aright, but an outward sign of those good things which a new country has produced for its people. . . . If poor, they are not abject in their poverty. They read and write. They walk like human beings made in God's form.[14]

Bagehot could never have felt anything like this. But Trollope with his novelist's passionate sense of the individual cannot ignore the fact of those individuals to whom the problems of survival are so demanding that ethics is an irrelevant luxury. 'Poverty makes the spirit poor, and the hands weak, and the heart sore,—and too often makes the conscience dull' (*Last Chronicle*, LXIX). Trollope is quite aware of the order of things even as described by Brecht, probably the best poet Marxism has ever had:

> *Erst* kommt das Fressen, *dann* kommt die Moral.

First comes the feeding, then you wise ones can tell us all about ethics. For now man so lives—

> Nur dadurch lebt der Mensch,
> Dass er so gründlich vergessen kann,
> Dass er ein Mensch doch ist—

that he can forget the very fact of his manhood.[15] It is the business of politics, and of propaganda novels, to get that big loaf of bread shared up aright. Trollope, however, does not write propaganda novels—not everyone could or should. He need not therefore be considered an uncharitable elitist, although he might agree with Bagehot that 'the character of the poor is an unfit subject for continuous art.'[16] But the fact that his Irish–American 'becomes more of a man' is of paramount importance. The dignity of man is a condition prerequisite to the ethical interest on which he builds his art.

As though in consequence, Trollope is a meliorist in politics, much more so than Bagehot is. But both know the necessity for reform, or both have a strong sense that reform to be safe must be slow. Both look on either side and know 'the doubtfulnesss things are involved in'—the phrase is Bishop Butler's, quoted by Bagehot.[17] *The Warden* is the paradigm of the doubtfulness Reform is involved in; Bagehot describes it referentially: 'We know, at least, that facts are many; that progress is complicated; that burning ideas (such as young men have) are mostly false and always incomplete.'[18] The machinery of government by which reform will and should come about, although formed from the 'select few,' is absurdly inadequate to the high purpose we traditionally ascribe to it. Both Bagehot and Trollope have a sense of the House of Commons as a 'club':

> ... if we think what a vast information, what a nice discretion, what a consistent will ought to mark the rules of that empire, we shall be surprised when we see them. We have a changing body of miscellaneous persons, sometimes few, sometimes many, never the same for an hour; sometimes excited, but mostly dull and half weary—impatient of eloquence, catching at any joke as an alleviation. . . . A cynical politician is said to have watched the long row of county members, so fresh and respectable-looking, and muttered, 'By Jove, they are the finest brute votes in Europe!'[19]

It is the fact that in all this changing and miscellaneous group there cannot be much devotion to principle. With such a group it would not work anyway; there are too many possible principles—or interest groups. 'A big meeting never does anything.' And yet the House of Commons is a big meeting, and does do things. The means to action is the party system. In it we see principle, and even selfish interest, sacrificed to party loyalty.

> The penalty of not doing so, is the penalty of impotence. It is not that you will not be able to do any good, but you will not be able to do anything at all. If everybody does what he thinks right, there will be 657 amendments to every motion, and none of them will be carried or the motion either.[20]

Here is a very Trollopian insight into a certain political truth; and Trollope makes great play on the moral ambiguities that arise from it. *At what point* does a man give up what he thinks right for the sake of effecting some action that may be partly right? Trollope will give us the cases. The problem involves that whole moral question Trollope takes up in his *Cicero*, too: principle and expediency. Even the good Parson of the Parish, as we saw, gives a little to the devil in order to gain more for God. By all this, we relearn the sad interdependency of good and evil.

The system gives rise to absurdities which are not only typical of human ethics, but may even have their actual uses. In the end of *The English Constitution* Bagehot makes his statement of what George Eliot calls her 'tenderness for old abuses,' and Trollope calls 'the sweet medieval flavour of old English corruption':[21]

> I own that I do not entirely sympathise with the horror of these anomalies which haunts some of our best critics. It is natural that those who by special and admirable culture have come to look at all things upon the artistic side, should start back from these queer peculiarities. But it is natural also that persons used to analyse political institutions should look at these anomalies with a little tenderness and a little interest. They *may* have something to teach us. Political philosophy is still more imperfect.[22]

That is, if the actuality is 'irrational,' the philosophy or the theory is still more so. To turn from Bagehot's *English Constitution* to Trollope's novels is to find the ironies of politics dramatised, and because they are dramatised in terms of recognisably human cases, Trollope goes deeper than Bagehot into the ethics of political man.

Trollope's *The Prime Minister* demonstrates his most important political situations, I think. It is the centre or focus of the series called Parliamentary, the Palliser novels, the series being united by the career of one of Trollope's best creations, Plantagenet Palliser, later Duke of Omnium. The other novels in the series have for their centres subjects other than Palliser himself. But through all the interweaving of affairs in the series—the panorama of overlapping social circles and social interdependencies, of purposes realised or frustrated, loves won or lost or changed, selves realised or doomed to impotence, lives of unimpeachable integrity, and utter blackguardism, but more of the ordinary mixtures, and then even a suicide and a murder—through all this arches the significant and beautifully realised story of Plantagenet Palliser and his wife, Lady Glencora. The concept of the series is surely one of the wonders of the century. And yet Trollope's stubborn understatement of it runs as follows:

> To carry out my scheme I have had to spread my picture over so wide a canvas that I cannot expect that any lover of such art should trouble himself to look at it as a whole. Who will read [the series] consecutively, in order that they may understand the characters of the Duke of Omnium, of Plantagenet Palliser, and of Lady Glencora? Who will ever know that they should be so read? . . . Taking him altogether, I think that Plantagenet Palliser stands more firmly on the ground than any other personage I have created.[23]

The novels that cover his career, this wide canvas, are surely the peak of Trollope's work. Where the Barchester novels sometimes give us a Dickensian caricature that is not in tone, or err too far on the side of farce, or suffer from their author's own overexuberant inventiveness, there is in the Palliser novels a surer touch, an economy, a restraint, and at the same time the broader range of a sophisticated and cultivated urban society.

Of all these novels, *The Prime Minister* is the one that centres most on Palliser himself, and on the great ironies of political life. Nineteenth-century English political history has in itself certain interesting ironies, and even the most cursory survey shows a striking incongruity: for the most part, liberal reform measures were actually passed and implemented under Tory administrations. So, although the party system is essential to political efficiency, party platforms seem to work in reverse.

> When some small measure of reform has thoroughly recommended itself to the country,—so thoroughly that all men know that the country will have it,—then the question arises whether its details shall be arranged by the political party which calls itself Liberal,—or by that which is termed Conservative. . . . 'See what we Conservatives can do. In fact we will conserve nothing when we find that you do not desire to have it conserved any longer' (*Phineas Redux*, XXXIII).

The irony still exists. Churchill was able to play on it in that election where he campaigned after Labour had in fact established the socialist state: 'Elect the Tories,' he said, 'and we'll show you how to really *run* socialism.' A somewhat similar irony exists in the mission of the Duke himself. Although as highly individuated as any character in nineteenth-century fiction, he is nevertheless a type also, a type of the Liberal English aristocrat whose high principles and sense of justice cause him, in effect, to implement the lessening of the distances between classes, a levelling that aims at a millennial idea. 'Equality would be a heaven, if we could attain it,' says the Duke.

> How can we to whom so much has been given dare to think otherwise? How can you look at the bowed back and bent legs and abject face of that poor ploughman . . . while you go a hunting . . .? You are a Liberal because you know that it is not all as it ought to be, and because you would still march on to some nearer approach to equality (LXVIII).

And so the great Liberal aristocrat himself presides over the demise of his class. It has its humour, and its pathos too, this situation. Trollope says of the old Duke of St. Bungay, Palliser's friend and adviser:

> There must surely have been a shade of melancholy on that old man's mind as, year after year, he assisted in pulling down institutions which he in truth regarded as the safeguards of the nation;—but which he knew that, as a Liberal, he was bound to assist in destroying (LXVIII).

There is a modern parallel again in the articulate Churchill, this time articulately wrong. It will be remembered that at a certain point after World War II he declared: 'I have not become the Queen's first minister in order to preside over the liquidation of the Empire.' But, as a matter of fact, he had.

The great liquidation of the old aristocratic régime, as of the old imperial régime, comes in good measure out of the very prevalence of *honestum,* from the Ciceronian ideal of the *gentleman,* fostered and maintained by upper class education. Part of the concept of the *gentleman* is that the work of government is the highest and most important work available. Thus Trollope:

> I have always thought that to sit in the British Parliament should be the highest object of ambition to every educated Englishman . . . that to serve one's country without pay is the grandest work that a man can do . . . —that of all studies the study of politics is the one in which a man may make himself most useful to his fellow creatures.[24]

And thus Cicero: 'For to that great God who rules all this world nothing is more acceptable than the meetings of counsellors for the service of the republic.'[25] The altruistic motive for running for Parliament is mixed with other motives, in Trollope, and in his characters. There is that feeling for Parliament as the best club in London, that gives you the highest status of all. There is also the pleasure of being in the know, of taking part in work which is indubitably worth the candle. Trollope acclaims this zest for politics in Cicero; Cicero loved Rome and loved being in the thick of things. He acclaims it too in Palmerston. When they offered to make Palmerston Lord Lieutenant of Ireland, or Governor General of India, writes Trollope,

> he laughed at the proposal. Not to be in the centre of everything,—at St. Stephen's, in Downing Street, in London where the Mayor and the Fishmongers had their banquets, ready for Greenwich dinners, ready for all attacks, for all explanations, for all discussions—was to him not to live.[26]

So, at the start, there is ambivalence of motive; the delight of the game is mixed up with the noble purpose.

One theme of *The Prime Minister* is the variety in motivation among members and prospective members. Of all those who stand for election in the novel, the Duke himself is the most disinterested and the most devoted to the public good. Among the others, motivation varies widely. Ferdinand Lopez, the scoundrel, requests financial support to stand, from his recalcitrant father-in-law. He requests it 'for Emily's sake.' That is, to have an M.P. for a husband would give position to Emily. The father-in-law objects:

> 'I don't think it would do Emily any good, or you either. It would certainly do me none. It is a kind of luxury that a man should not attempt to enjoy unless he can afford it easily.'
> 'A luxury!'
> 'Yes, a luxury; just as much as a four-in-hand coach or a yacht. Men go into Parliament because it gives them fashion, position, and power.'
> 'I should go to serve my country.'
> 'Success in your profession I thought you said was your object' (xxix).

His real motive is to manipulate the stock market for his own gain. Everett Wharton has a glimmer of principle in seeking office for himself and thinks he is guided by it. But he is not clever enough to obscure his more selfish motives: 'Consider what a parliamentary education would be to me!' (xxii). Arthur Fletcher might be one of that 'long row of county members, so fresh and respectable-looking' that Bagehot's cynical observer called the 'finest brute votes in Europe'; and yet though Arthur is typical in many ways of the Tory landed gentry (whereas the aristocrats like the Duke were more often Whig), he is not stupid. His older brother John has the finer intellect, but Arthur has by education, and by his birthright as a gentleman, and by his certainly adequate intellect, all the qualifications to make him an ideal M.P. And as traditions go, there is nothing more natural to a man of his class and type than to stand for Parliament. It is matter of course, and represents no finely considered calculation, nor any high flown idealism either. More specifically, he is persuaded to stand for office partly to distract himself from his disappointment in love. Even the women's motivations are closely anatomised: Glencora herself wants her husband in power for love of him, for the dignity of it, and also for her own love of power. She would see herself as a great intriguer, and manipulator of men and factions.

But the quality of motivation does not necessarily control the quality of the government. Such is the machinery of party and opposition, and the power of the press and public opinion, that things get done, somehow, and a measure is passed, and in Phineas's words to the Duke, there has been made 'a step towards a step to the millennium' (LXXIII).

The work of Parliament is still the grandest work a man can do, but the means to do it is less than grand. Briggs writes:

> Like Bagehot, Trollope was conscious of the honour of becoming a member of Parliament, of belonging to the inner circle of the political elite; but he realised that elections were, a somewhat unsatisfactory means of getting into Parliament, because they were sordid and corrupt exercises in bribery, cajolery, and violence rather than rational verdicts of the local will. . . . The way to the Palace of Westminster led through a pig-sty.[27]

The elections in *The Prime Minister*, with all their grubby financial machinations, demonstrate the point. But the best demonstration is perhaps in *Ralph the Heir*, where Sir Thomas Underwood's campaign reflects more closely than any other Trollope's actual campaign experience in Beverley, as he himself says.[28] Trollope makes an interesting change, however, in order, I believe, to sharpen the ironic situation. Though Sir Thomas Underwood is like himself in his general attitude, he makes him a Conservative where Trollope himself had stood as a Liberal. The situation is amusing and pregnant: Underwood, the Conservative, and Ontario Moggs, the Radical, are quite alike in uprightness and in their horror of the well-established tradition of bribery and corruption in the constituency. The other candidates, Westmacott and Griffenbottom, are old in the ways of politics and have long ago come to terms with the corrupt practices. But old Tory

Underwood and young Radical Moggs are both babes in the contest, naïvely trusting they may stand out against the free beer and the shillings. We see Trollope heightening the irony of things again, by denying that right and justice belong exclusively on any one side; the extreme left is just as honest in this as the extreme right.

But the most significant truths of political life are dramatised in the character of Plantagenet Palliser himself, and most clearly so in *The Prime Minister*. The controlling theme is this: the Duke is as excellent a man as one can imagine—no one could be more dedicated to his country's good, no one have a greater honesty and higher principles—and yet he fails as Prime Minister precisely because of his goodness.

He comes into office to head a coalition, always a *faute de mieux* government in a parliamentary system, which in actuality occurred rather often in Trollope's time. For by it, the party system, which is the engine, is frustrated. And Palliser heads this coalition, *faute de mieux*, also; neither Mr. Gresham nor Mr. Daubeny, both acknowledgedly more effective, has been able to form a government. The Duke really knows all this and feels inadequate; yet he takes up his office with modest pride and a high sense of mission, and a sense of the 'heaven' of that political millennium toward which the country must move, by slow and cautious steps. He has 'rank, and intellect, and parliamentary habits . . . and unblemished, unextinguishable, inexhaustible love of country . . . as the ruling principle of his life.'[29] But this is not enough. He has certain qualities of character that, in themselves virtuous, disqualify him as an executive. He lacks the geniality that a leader needs; the power of attracting friends to him and holding them: 'he knew that he was saturnine and silent, and that it behooved him as a leader of men to be genial and communicative' (LVI). On such things may our political weal depend, absurdly enough, on 'how thoroughly men may be alienated by silence and a cold demeanour' (LXXIII), rather than by opportunism or stupidity or dishonesty. That

original sense he had of his inadequacy for his high office
sprang from his modest sense of intellectual or moral inadequacy; he felt he could not be a great man. And yet his
real inadequacy is his greatness. He is so high principled,
so scrupulous, that he will not bend. Though his principles
lead ultimately towards democracy, too, his taste is aristocratic, and therefore part of the horror of public life for him
turns on his horror of vulgarity. Glencora his wife has a much
surer sense of how one must bend to the vulgar herd, and she
is in her adorably witty way only too ready to do so. In her
attempts to support him by so bending, however, she goes too
far and brings her husband's censure on her head, and also
the painful accusation of 'vulgarity.' In the chapter called
'Vulgarity,' the Duchess muses on the accusation, or fumes,
rather. And we must sympathise with both husband and wife,
in their offended sensibilities.

> When a man wants to be Prime Minister he has to submit to
> vulgarity, and must give up his ambition if the task be too
> disagreeable to him. The Duchess thought that that had been
> understood, at any rate since the days of Coriolanus. . . . 'He
> wants it to be done. And when I do it for him because he can't
> do it for himself, he calls it by an ugly name!' (xix).

The reference to Coriolanus is not insignificant. The political
problem of Shakespeare's play is very like the one that is the
issue here in Victorian guise. There is also an element of
Shakespeare's Brutus in the Duke. In his notes on *Julius
Caesar*, Trollope records his opinion that Brutus is perhaps
Shakespeare's finest character (just as he feels Palliser is his
own finest), and he admires in the characterisation 'the
honesty of the man and the ill adaptation of [it] to political
exigencies.'[30] The Duke will not bend in manner for a vote or a
favourable press, or even for that party solidarity without
which nothing.

The association with vulgarity, however, is for the Duke not
much of a horror compared with the association with downright immorality. Having to be allied with a shady broker

like Ferdinand Lopez, is unbearable. All the trouble with
Lopez arises in that borough which had in the old days been
pocket borough of the Dukes of Omnium. Pocket boroughs
are now, of course, reformed, and the Duke is most meticulous
to stay aloof from the election there; and yet such is the
tendency of the electorate to toady to a great man, and so
eager is the Duchess to aid her husband, that she lets fall
a word of commitment, and the Duke has a devil of a time to
keep the borough out of his pocket. Even if it were to the
country's advantage, *he* would not have let that word fall.
He will not look to results, but will do right as he sees it.
He is 'always right in his purpose,' then, 'but generally wrong
in his practice.' He is altogether too honest. The Duchess
complains of his contrariety: 'He never wants to say anything
unless he has got something to say!' She complains, and
adores too. 'He is all trust, even when he knows that he is
being deceived. He is honour complete from head to foot. Ah,'
she continues, talking to her close friend Mrs. Finn, 'it was
before you knew me when I tried him hardest . . . he behaved
like a god' (LVI). She refers back to that old incident of long
ago when she came close to running off with the attractive
and very bending Burgo Fitzgerald. It is an interesting reference, for it reminds us of the Palliser's boundless generosity,
as Glencora reminds herself. He is too good, perhaps;
too good for political life, certainly. He is horrified when the
practised politician, Sir Orlando Drought, proposes to him
that 'we should try and arrange among ourselves something
of a policy—' for political advantage, of course. The Duke
dryly reproves him: 'Things to be done offer themselves, I
suppose, because they are in themselves desirable; not because
it is desirable to have something to do' (XXII). Trollope's own
feeling for the Duke's point comes out strongly when he tells
his own story in the *Autobiography*:

> It was a matter for study to see how at Beverley politics were
> appreciated because they might subserve electoral purposes,
> and how little it was understood that electoral purposes,

which are in themselves a nuisance, should be endured in order that they might subserve politics.[31]

Trollope did study it, and he presents it here—not with the bitterness of the defeated candidate for Beverley—but he presents it, may one say, recollected in tranquillity? Certainly we can say it is presented with the intelligent control of ironic humour. Sir Orlando Drought and his damnable popular platform of four new men-of-war, which are of no use to the country whatsoever, but might be of use as a political manoeuvre, persist through the remainder of the Duke's term of office, to his great indignation. And yet to study English constitutional history of the century is to discover, as Briggs puts it, that 'the reform bills of ministers were less triumphant vindications of principle than useful political manoeuvres.'[32] It is as well to know this fact of history; and it is as profitable as it is delightful to see it acted out in Trollope's novel, especially since the quaint practices of the Victorians have, some of them, survived.

The Duke had hoped to lead the country on reasoned moral principles, to enact measures 'in themselves desirable.' We find him after some few months in office, sitting alone contemplating his discoveries, and, Trollope says, 'conscientiously endeavouring to define for himself, not a future policy, but the past policy of the last month or two' (xviii). His anxiety is now that the choosing of himself as Prime Minister has itself been only a useful manoeuvre. It is horrible to him that he may be known as a *fainéant*, and he pines for those days when he had real work to do, with figures and papers and committees and plans, for—say—currency reform. It seems he must now learn all sorts of practices that seem to him altogether unethical. His government must, it appears, pretend to more unity than it has. Sir Orlando had declared in the House that the government had been 'quite in unison' on the question of county suffrage, although in fact it was much divided. The Prime Minister expresses his dismay to the old Duke of St. Bungay.

'If there be differences of opinion they must be kept in the background,' said the Duke of St. Bungay.

'Nothing can justify a direct falsehood,' said the Duke of Omnium (xxxvii).

Bagehot had told a story in *The English Constitution* which Trollope no doubt noted.

> It is *said* that at the end of the Cabinet which agreed to propose a fixed duty on corn, Lord Melbourne put his back to the door and said, 'Now is it to lower the price of corn or isn't it? It is not much matter which we say, but mind, we must all say the *same*.'[33]

Bagehot and Trollope knew that things like this have to happen, but our Duke cannot bear the dishonesty of it.

On the occasion when Sir Orlando's four men-of-war have indeed proved useful as an issue by which to manipulate the House, and to weaken the Duke's government, the Duke's heart is nearly broken. He declares to his adviser:

> 'When I see a man who is supposed to have earned the name of statesman, and been high in the councils of his sovereign, induced by personal jealousy to do as he is doing, it makes me feel that an honest man should not place himself where he may have to deal with such persons.' 'According to that [counters St. Bungay] the honest men are to desert their country in order that the dishonest men may have everything their own way.' Our Duke could not answer this (LVI).

He could not because he had not faced these moral ambivalences of politics as Cicero had. 'Without that evil you cannot have the good which the institution contains.'[34] That one must at least associate with the evil is the awful problem of the honest man in public office. Mere honesty is not enough. The two Dukes are in the Upper House listening to that foolish man Lord Fawn whom we have met in previous novels, and the following whispered exchange takes place:

> ST. BUNGAY: 'He has a wonderful gift of saying nothing with second-rate dignity.'

OMNIUM: 'A very honest man.'
ST. BUNGAY: 'A sort of bastard honesty,—by precept out of stupidity' (LVI).

Of course it is witty, like so much of the talk in this whole series of novels; and it is also, like the best wit, rich in substance. In this little remark Trollope's deflation of the limited usefulness of any precept comes out clear; even honesty will not be useful if there is not some intelligence with it. And it takes intelligence to find the right relationship of principle to practice in each case. Near the end of the book the Prime Minister himself admonishes Phineas Finn, who is actually much more the realist than himself: 'These moral speculations, Mr. Finn, will hardly bear the wear and tear of real life' (LXXII). It is with a sadly acquired wisdom that the Duke speaks, a wisdom that he was himself unable to apply.

So the Duke does fail as Prime Minister through his very goodness. A leader must not be thin-skinned like our Duke —who can endure neither criticism nor bad opinion. He must, clearly, sacrifice some part of principle for a larger good. Trollope has one passage in this novel where he acclaims dear 'old Brock' who was a successful leader for many years, and who is pretty clearly a picture of Lord Palmerston (XLI). And in his book on Palmerston he is even more clear: Palmerston was successful because he was *not* a genius and his followers could always understand him.[35] His 'great merit as a governing man arose from his perfect sympathy with those whom he was called upon to govern.'[36] Compare Bagehot, on how Palmerston 'was not a common man, but a common man might be cut out of him.'[37] In a way, it does not much matter who is Prime Minister—Smith may be very good, but Jones will do as well. Palmerston was thick-skinned, resilient and tireless in the mêlée of affairs.

As our Duke's ministry draws to a close, we find him, even him, succumbing to the evils that power makes. He becomes somewhat bitter and cantankerous, and stages a little rebellion against the rules. By time-honoured custom, the Prime Minister has in his gift the Order of the Garter, and this has always been part of the spoils system, and will be awarded wherever there may be the most political advantage. The Duke, contrarily, is determined to show that 'he owes nothing and will pay nothing,' and he awards the order on no basis other than merit. He searches out and selects a certain Lord Earlybird who has, with a moderate fortune, done much on his own to improve the housing and education of the labouring man. He is of no political importance whatsoever. The pain and distress of the Duke's associates is only matched by the utter astonishment of old Lord Earlybird. For his pains, the Duke is considered 'quixotic' by his friends, and an unfriendly press asserts that he has been 'guilty of a pretentious love of virtue.' This is the extent to which Palliser is corrupted by power (LXVI).

When the end of the administration is in sight, Phineas Finn tries to reassure the Duke. 'After all,' he says, 'the innings has not been a bad one. It has been of service to the country, and has lasted longer than most men expected' (LXVIII). But the Duke had wanted it to be so much more; had wanted his government to have distinguished itself in the service of his country. Instead, he must be content with having merely kept things going, in a coalition-y, compromise-y, *fainéant* sort of way. In due course, the good man bows out. Another good politician, but a tougher one, begs that he will not altogether give up the business of government. And the Duke humbles himself, characteristically modest and dutiful, and looks to a time when he may again be of use, at a committeee level. A noble aspiration is frustrated by its very nobility, and this particular drama of political man—man in society—is closed. Bagehot writes, in sympathy with the relativism of Trollope: 'Politics are made in time and place—institutions are shifting things to be tried and adjusted to the shifting conditions of a moveable world.'[38] And men in their relationships to their institutions define themselves in strangely ambivalent ways. A selfish or a stupid motivation may result in a public good, and a noble aspiration may result in something less.

And yet the mere existence of goodness such as Plantagenet Palliser's is enormously important. He fails as Prime Minister, but how he triumphs morally, and how he triumphs in art, as an assertion of the Trollopian sense of the possibilities for decency!

The great series is rounded out in the last Palliser novel, *The Duke's Children*.[39] Where *The Prime Minister* shows the Duke's problems as political man, *The Duke's Children* shows him as parent, faced with the specific cases of his own two elder children and their maturing and courtships. The mutual love of the children and the father is very deep, and it is sad that, in Hagan's words, 'with all this love on both sides, father and son must equally destroy for a time the other's happiness.'[40] John H. Hagan shows how Trollope points the irony in little dramatic situations as when young Silverbridge reproves his sister Mary for distressing their father by permitting Tregear's courtship, while he himself creates a greater distress for the father by immediately falling in love with the American Isabel Boncassen. He points out the comic irony in Isabel— how although so republican in principle she is very susceptible to a Lord. He points out a more important and more beautiful comic irony in the character of the Duke himself—how he obscures his own true lovable nobility with his characteristic pompous sententiousness. Furthermore, Hagan gives due emphasis to the contrast between the Duke's grand political liberalism, and how he will not apply the theory to his own family. This brings us to the relevance this book has to the whole Palliser series. Just as the great Liberal aristocrat presides over the dissolution of the system that made him great, so now in the matter of his own family, the Duke is driven—in these painfully pressing cases—to consistency, and he at last must give in to Silverbridge's marriage to the American, and Lady Mary's marriage to the penniless gentleman. For neither marriage is wrong according to his own high principles. In such a way this novel rounds out the political whole of the Palliser series.

But there is another strain that is completed here: the story of Palliser's own private life—of how Glencora chafed at the marriage, such a 'good' marriage, but he so dull and wise and unromantic, how she nearly ran off with the devilishly attractive Burgo Fitzgerald, and how nobly Palliser forgave her, and though hurt, and aware of his dullness, how tenderly he loved her, and adored her mercurial brilliance, however trying it was, and how she in spite of her teasing and baiting of the man, knew really how he relished her wit, and how he countered with occasional sallies of his own, not nearly as often as he would wish to have done.

In the opening of *The Duke's Children* she is dead, and readers may find themselves nostalgic for her delightful company. The Duke is at a loss without her, especially when he finds on his hands the difficult problems of the children. He adores her memory, and still suffers from her mischief. She, it appears, had sanctioned Lady Mary's friendship with Tregear, which the Duke deplores. We, and the Duke himself, are aware of the parallel between the Glencora–Fitzgerald and Mary–Tregear relationships, and so in a way the Duke must still deal with the Fitzgerald problem. By what difficult trials he must overcome his political prejudices and his sexual prejudices to at last sanction both marriages is the delicate psychological and moral stuff of this novel. He failed as Prime Minister, insofar as what he hoped for could not be realised. He fails as a parent in preventing unsuitable marriages. But as Prime Minister he was victorious, too: he did keep the government going, he did maintain his high principles, and he successfully resisted the temptations of power, by admitting his inadequacies for leadership. As a parent he is ultimately victorious too, victorious over himself as he extends his high principle of liberalism to these cases that touch him so nearly; he embraces as daughter-in-law the republican granddaughter of a labourer, and he is victorious over his own old jealousy of Fitzgerald when he sanctions the true love of Lady Mary and Tregear.

The Palliser series is, I suppose, Trollope's *magnum opus,* and yet there is such abundance of richness outside it, one hesitates to say so. But the series has a greatness like that of Balzac's *Comédie Humaine,* and there are grounds on which one might rank Trollope's work higher. With Plantagenet and Glencora as focal centre, these novels extend in scope to the whole matter of man in society: from his largest social context, which is political, to his most intimate social context, which is in this case a marriage.

NOTES

[1]Chapter XVI.

[2]*The English Constitution*, printed in full, pp. 192–401, in *Walter Bagehot*, by Norman St. John-Stevas. Indiana University Press, Bloomington; and Eyre & Spottiswoode, London, 1959.

[3]'Trollope, Bagehot, and the English Constitution,' in *Victorian People.*

[4]Gertrude Himmelfarb, reviewing Bagehot's *Historical Essays*. Garden City, New York, 1965, in *New York Review of Books*, iv, May 6, 1965, 18–19.

[5]*The English Constitution*, p. 244.

[6]P. 204.   [7]*Walter Bagehot,* p. 27.   [8]*Autobiography,* p. 243.   [9]P. 255.   [10]P. 251.

[11]P. 240.   [12]P. 388.

[13]*North America*, ed. D. Smalley and B. A. Booth. New York, Alfred A. Knopf, 1951, pp. 136–137.

[14]Pp. 527–528.

[15]Bertolt Brecht, *Die Dreigroschenoper*, Universal Edition, Vienna, 1928 pp. 54–55. My paraphrase. The italics are not so much mine as Kurt Weil's,i n that music which gives the lines their perfect emphasis.

[16]Quoted in *Victorian People*, p. 94.

[17]*The English Constitution*, p. 275.

[18]P. 276.   [19]Pp. 308–311.   [20]P. 311.

[21]*Clergymen of the Church of England*, p. 28.

[22]*The English Constitution*, p. 400.

[23]*Autobiography*, pp. 154–155.

[24]Pp. 242–243.

[25]This passage is from Trollope's own translation of that famous part of Cicero's *De Republica*, Book V I, Section V I I, which is called 'Scipio's Dream.' Its appeal is perennial, and it is in itself notable for irony. Chaucer uses it at the end of the *Troilus*, for the vantage ground of truth from which Troilus looks down on 'this litel spot of erthe,' 'this wretched world,' and 'he lough.' It affords the ironic overview, and perhaps this is why it so takes Chaucer and Trollope. Trollope appends his own translation of the whole of it to his *Cicero*, and quotes the passage I quote in my text here in 'Cicero as a man of Letters,' an article he wrote for *The Fortnightly Review*, x x v ɹ, September 1, 1877, 401–422.

[26]*Lord Palmerston*. London, William Isbister, 1882, p. 9.

[27]*Victorian People*, pp. 99–100.

[28]*Autobiography*, p. 285.

[29]P. 299.

[30]*Trollope on the Old Drama*, notes on *Julius Caesar*.

[31]*Autobiography*, p. 253

[32]*Victorian People*, p. 90.

[33]Note, *The English Constitution*, p. 236.

[34]*Cicero*, ɪɪ, 311; and above, Chapter I I.

[35]*Lord Palmerston*, pp. 46–47.

[36]P. 200.

[37]Quoted in *Walter Bagehot*, p. 32.

[38]Quoted in *Victorian People*, p. 112.

[39]On this novel, John H. Hagan who to my mind misses the point so grievously in the matter of *The Warden* (see above, Chapter I I, note 1), has written an illuminating study demonstrating not only the novel's excellence in itself but also its relevance to the series. ('*The Duke's Children:* Trollope's Psychological Masterpiece,' *N C F*, xɪɪ, June, 1958, 1–21.) Here, he errs only, I think, in claiming that this novel is somewhat singular for its insight. There are so very many of Trollope's novels where closer and closer examination reveals more and more brilliance of psychological understanding. Perhaps as one novel and then another is accorded the fine analysis Hagan gives *The Duke's Children* here, and Thale gives *The Last Chronicle* elsewhere (see above, Chapter I I, note 10)—as such studies accumulate—then perhaps will be established some sort of broad generalisation about Trollope, and we will not be so utterly surprised by his art in any one novel.

[40]P. 5.

Chapter VII

SIC VIVITUR

Sic multa quae honesta natura videntur esse, temporibus
fiunt non honesta.

CICERO, *De Officiis*

The virtues of one generation will be the vices of another.

TROLLOPE, *La Vendée*

As a by-product of the Age of Reform, the novelist finds
to hand certain interesting anomalies, and when dramatic-
ally set off these anomalies engage us and demand of us new—
and adjustable—perspectives. But the Age of Reform is only
an ordinary sort of age in that it is only one phase of that
Heraclitean fire which is our sole constant. That it was called
the Age of Reform indicates a special consciousness of the
flux and perpetual readjustment, and perhaps a heightening
of pace in the process itself. The new words *relativity*
and *relativism* are an index of that consciousness of change.
Indeed one cannot think for long of Man as an unchanging
absolute; he barely exists except socially, in relation to
actual conventions and institutions, and it is these which
change. The work of defining is always to be done anew,
the defining of personality and convention in terms of each
other.

Trollope's novels can be thought of as multidimensional
assessments of men in terms of Church and Parliament, and of
those institutions in terms of his own vivid sense of the
Victorian *comment c'est*. Church and Parliament in his most
famous novels, that is, and other conventions in other novels.
The range is very great, and the studies very objective. He
throws his *lumen siccus* on the English class system, on
primogeniture, on the law, on courtship and marriage, on

finance, and then finally on patriotism and Empire and internationalism.

Marion Fay is a little-known late novel (1882) that centres especially on the English classes, the hierarchy and its inter-relationships. It is taken for granted here, as in the other novels, that there is a slow levelling process going on. Lord Hampstead, heir to an ancient title and fortune, is a thought-ful and moral young man who on logical and moral grounds would change the whole system to a 'communistic' one. He even refuses to run for Parliament because he has scruples about taking part in a government one of whose chambers is an hereditary one. But literate and fair-minded and objective as he is, nevertheless when it comes to his own family, his principles shift a little. His sister Fanny falls in love with an intelligent young Post Office clerk, George Roden, whom Hampstead himself has brought home as part of his democ-ratising programme. Hampstead cannot approve the alliance. Then he himself falls in love with Marion Fay, a Quaker of humble station, and his principles have to accommodate themselves the other way, to this other case. It now seems that it is more permissible for an aristocratic man to stoop in marriage than for an aristocratic woman. Hampstead does not invent this fact to suit his inclinations, he only discovers it. It was, I think, indeed true in the England of his time that there were fewer obstacles to a successful marriage when the man married beneath him than when the woman did. Hamp-stead seems an acute observer of society, an intelligent political scientist, and because at the same time he seems as unselfish as a man can be—without being a saint—we are the more interested in how in his case the selfish ends are to be adjusted to the unselfish. He involves his father in political disquisi-tions, and his father finds the disquisitions far too long. He was a liberal himself in his youth and has now turned Estab-lishment, feeling he has settled these things once for all. But for the reader, these things are not settled, and Hampstead's speeches are not at all too long. Trollope maintains the double ironic view: on the one hand Hampstead amuses and delights us, and on the other he commands our attention as one of Trollope's most articulate intellectuals, and spokesman for much of what may be Trollope's own opinions.

'*Noblesse oblige*,' his father the Marquis says to him, as he tries to gain the son's support in absolutely separating Fanny from Roden. Hampstead answers:

> I do acknowledge that as very much has been given to me in the way of education, of social advantages, and even of money, a higher line of conduct is justly demanded from me than from those who have been less gifted. So far, *noblesse oblige*. But before I undertake the duty thus imposed upon me, I must find out what is the higher line of conduct. Fanny should do the same (x).

Hampstead, like Trollope, is now the careful Ciceronian casuist.

One anomaly in this study of class levels is that although Hampstead is steadfastly republican he himself happens to embody everything that is lovely about the old aristocracy —the urbanity and social grace, the easy manners that can even be called democratic, and the moral awareness that education in itself sometimes imparts. George Roden, his good friend and intellectual equal, is quite acceptable in his manners, but Roden's fellow clerk, Crocker, is everything that is dreadful in his class. Hampstead is obliged to endure him on principle, though he hates him. But if something morally reprehensible turns up, as it does in the chaplain Mr. Greenwood, why then Hampstead says that in comparison he *loves* Crocker. Trollope does not spare us, however, the horror of Crocker's vulgarity, some of which consists in abject grovelling before a title. The dreary lower-middle class appears briefly as the Fays' neighbours in 'Paradise Row'; we see enough of them to know we wish the Fays and Rodens did not have to consort with them. Other novels give us a taste of this level of society: for example, there is a wonderfully drab lower-middle-class household in *Miss Mackenzie*, the household on Arundel Street; and there is a wonderfully drab lower-middle-class mind in Mrs. Masters, in *The American Senator*. The masses Trollope generally neglects, with some exceptions like the Brattles in *The Vicar of Bullhampton*, who are excellently done, and other rustics more or less comic, like Ruby Ruggles in *The Way We Live Now*, who are not well done. In this book there is a Welsh lord, arch-Conservative in contrast to Hampstead; although not very bright he is nevertheless a good and disinterested man, and useful to his country. Hampstead's friend Vivian is an aristocrat of no apparent use at all. He is charmingly light-minded and quite insouciant as to Hampstead's altruism. The friendship is nevertheless firm, and delightful for the rather Oscar Wildean talk.

The least pleasant contrast to Hampstead's egalitarianism is exemplified in his stepmother. It is the grief of her life that none of her own young sons can accede to the title. She is jealous of Hampstead personally, and yet over-deferential to him as The Heir. In title-worshipping she is hardly better than the dreadful Crocker. She disapproves in her jealousy the mutual adoration between Hampstead and her three little boys. Hampstead is inclined to tease this hard and humour-less woman: once, having routed one of the boys out of bed for a romp, and feeling the woman's cold eye on him, he remarks loud and clear to his father the Marquis, 'Nothing does children so much good as disturbing them in their sleep!' (xi.) These scenes of play are briefly done (ix and xi), but you can almost hear the loud delighted laughter of those little lords in their night-shirts, as Hampstead tosses them up in the air. I think the concept of their titles is being tossed up in the air, too.

The denouement of the story is a shameless *deus ex machina*, and we cannot call this novel one of Trollope's best, for this reason and also for the over-distressing death of Marion Fay. All the same, the *deus ex machina* makes a fine humorous point. George Roden, the humble Post Office clerk with just a touch of mystery in his origin, suddenly inherits a title, and so becomes happily eligible to marry Hampstead's sister. But the title he inherits is of a specific kind that shows up the absurdity of titles *per se*. First, it is only a title. Not a penny comes with it. Without means to support it there seems very little point in it. Second, it is an *Italian* title; Roden is now a *Duca*. The English suspicion of things foreign implies something about titles in general. As an Englishman turns up his nose at an Italian title as being somehow invalid, it would seem that English titles must be valid only because they are English. Which is not firm grounds for supporting a system of titles.

In *Mr. Scarborough's Family* it is not hereditary aristocracy that is the convention at issue, but the related matter of primogeniture and the laws that support it. Trollope chooses a peculiar case that forces the issue into new light, and that, as usual, raises rather than answers questions. Mr. Scarborough is an interestingly amoral character who takes a pleasure in outwitting the law: by clever manipulation he succeeds in turning the moral purpose of the law upside down while keeping well within the letter of it. He has legal records of two marriages to his late wife, and, depending on which record he chooses to produce, may make his heir whichever he wishes of his two sons. If the later record stands, the elder son is a bastard, the younger is the heir. All this tends to make primogeniture in itself look absurd, since it can be so manipulated.

It also puts an equivocal light on the law itself, as such. Mr. Grey, Scarborough's lawyer, is everything that is good in the law, especially as aided by his daughter Dolly. Dolly is something of a specialist in moral philosophy, and is her father's trusted adviser in tricky moral decisions. She can in fact see the law's limitations better than her father. He calls her the 'conscience' of the firm, and her charm and forthright wit suggest what pleasant company a 'conscience' can be. There is much pathos in how the upright lawyer is hoodwinked

by the unscrupulous Scarborough. 'The light that has guided
me through my professional life has been a love of the law,'
says Grey when he sees how it is. 'I am sure that the law and
justice may be made to run on all fours. . . . The chance has
brought me into the position of having for a client a man the
passion of whose life has been the very reverse' (LV). All
this brings us back to Trollope's Ciceronian strain of thought:
man is 'natus ad justitiam'—born with an idea of justice—as
the beasts are not. And law is the human effort to effect that
justice. It is an effort to generalise, then; to set up precepts
that will apply to as many cases as possible. And yet, as
Trollope is so often concerned to point out, no generalisation
will ever hold in all cases, no precept will serve at all times.
Trollope explores this case where the worthiest social effort
of man, the law, which aims to effect that human ideal of
justice—even the law—is signally inadequate. It has taken
an extreme variation to produce such a case. Mr. Scarborough
is a most extraordinary man, with the most superior intellectual powers to turn to his doubtful ends. There is a contrasting, contrapuntal case in the book, another inheritance:
Harry Annesley, the good-hearted 'hero' of the story, has
long been chosen the heir of his wealthy bachelor uncle, who
is an ass, and who takes up a scrape of Harry's as an excuse for
disinheriting him. Or, it is supposed to be a scrape; 'He thinks
that he is quarrelling with you about that affair in London,
but it is in truth because you have declined to hear him read
his sermons' (XIV). Harry's father comments:

> 'It is dreadful to have to depend on a fool,—to have to
> trust to a man who cannot tell wrong from right. Your uncle
> intends to be a good man. . . . He would not rob. . . . But he
> is a fool, and he does not know when he is doing these things'
> (XXV).

The *virtù* and intelligence of Scarborough stand in contrast
with this stupidity. He has a kind of principle of his own
that demands respect. When he dies at last, the young doctor
who knew him well writes of him:

Mr. Grey condemns him, and all the world must condemn him. One cannot make an apology for him without being ready to throw all truth and morality to the dogs. But if you can imagine for yourself a state of things in which neither truth nor morality shall be thought essential, then old Mr. Scarborough would be your hero. He was the bravest man I ever knew. . . . And whatever he did he did with the view of accomplishing what he thought to be right for other people (LXIII).

We, knowing the history of his actions, have to concur. So even here, there is a case wherein 'right and truth lie on neither side exclusively.' Dolly, hating Scarborough's morals, had always wanted her father to cease serving him. Dolly, the 'conscience,' is said often to be a 'good hater.' Law is not enough, then: we need a passionate hatred of turpitude. There is a virtuoso quality in the way Trollope manipulates this case, insisting on its complexity and difficulty, insisting on moral relativism—we must realise Harry's uncle's unconscious selfishness is in some respects more reprehensible than Scarborough's fraud. And the oddness of this barely believable case demands a situation ethic.

Is He Popenjoy? is another brilliant variation on the theme of primogeniture, along with hereditary position in general. The nature of the ironic deflation in this book is that Trollope brings the whole noble subject down to questions of bastardy and pregnancy and sexual honesty on which it does in truth depend. One remembers Gibbon saying he never interested himself much in the study of lineage as history, because the whole business of lineage depends only on the honesty of the female, and Gibbon has not much faith in *that*. Now Trollope has, although of course it is his nature to discriminate: in this book Mary Germain deserves all our trust—it would be nonsense to think of her as possibly adulterous, while it would be equally nonsensical to trust the Marquis's Italian concubine. This novel turns, as the title implies, on the identity of the true heir. The Marquis of Brotherton is a malcontent who has lived a shady life on the continent, and he brings home to

England with him an Italian woman and an infant son, sickly, dark, and generally very un-English, whom he declares to be the heir. The interest is in whether this poor creature is in truth the heir, or a bastard; or is the heir actually the problematical because as yet unconceived son of the younger brother Lord George Germain and his wife Mary? Mary has stumbled rather blindly into her marriage with Lord George, mostly because of her father, the Dean of Brotherton, one of Trollope's 'worldly' clergymen. The Dean comes from a little below the class on which the Church generally draws for its gentlemen, and he is always anxious to establish his gentility, and is somewhat over-excited at the possibility of being grandfather to a Marquis.

The novel has a great deal of interest for the way in which, although it depends on things for which the terms are, in fact, *bastard, pregnancy,* and *whore,* Trollope is not at all hampered by conventions of Victorian decorum. It is rather that he turns all the prudery to his advantage. A great deal of the humour, and the human interest, arises from the fact that these things which are of the most painfully urgent concern to his characters cannot be really named by them. It is fairly late Trollope—1875—a time when propriety was a little looser than it had been; so that one of his characters can say, 'The time is gone when men, or women either, were too qualmish and too queasy to admit the truth even to themselves' (xxix). Trollope in this, as in politics and religion, is much aware of the changefulness of things that we know so well, as we have seen license in literature slowly broaden down from precedent to precedent. But of course 1875 is not 1970, and I think even *Popenjoy* could have been read in the Victorian family circle. The interesting thing is how, even so, Trollope can say so much. For instance, it is pretty clear that the Marquis is syphilitic: enough of his dissolute career is suggested, his behaviour is insane enough, and his off-spring is sickly enough for the adult reader to draw conclusions. But the Young Person will be quite satisfied only to think him a

brute. Trollope makes humorous use of the evasion of
'bastard': when the Dean says to his daughter: 'If this child
be—anything else than what he pretends to be, there will be
fraud' (xvi), we smile to think that the poor sickly infant
could have 'pretenses.' It is clear that when the Marquis
visits the Dean and insults his daughter, accusing her of
adultery with Jack de Baron, he uses the word *whore*; we can
be sure because we know that the Dean flies in the face of his
own gentility and the Marquis's title, by both of which he sets
such great store, and with the strong sinews inherited from
the livery stable proprietor his father, flings the Marquis
into the fireplace so that his head is seriously bashed in. When
help comes the Marquis luckily repeats the insult in front of
witnesses, from his painful position against the iron grate.
'"She is a —— [sic]," said the imprudent prostrate Marquis.
The Sergeant, the doctor who was now present, and Mrs.
Walker [the landlady] suddenly became the Dean's friends'
(xli). The Dean, however, is too proud to repeat the insult
to his son-in-law, and therefore the son-in-law, Lord George,
never quite believes the Marquis said it, and so harbours some
resentment against the Dean. Mary says to her husband,
'Surely you wouldn't let me go anywhere where such names as
that are believed against me?' and Trollope adds, 'She had not
heard the name, nor had he, and they were in the dark' (xliv).

Mary finds herself pregnant. This piece of news, which can
barely be mentioned with propriety, creates vast changes in
the attitudes of everybody. The Dean her father, though
inwardly doing handstands for joy, rises to new accesses of
dignified gentility; Lord George's proud sisters, who had
found the Dean vulgar, come to appreciate his essential
warmth and piety, and they accord Mary the right to abstain
from their sordid philanthropic work among the poor; Lord
George forgives all past annoyances; and Mary herself—well,
Mary is appalled by all those baby clothes that appear, each
item with a coronet. But we feel sure she has succeeded in
defining her role securely.

The comedy is all played off against the absurdities of hereditary titles, but in one sense the story has been all Mary's, and is in this sense a comment on another political question, the Woman Question. Mary marries very young barely out of school, swayed by her father's predilection for Lord George's title; and Lord George, in turn, stoops in station for the sake of the Dean's money as well as Mary's grace and prettiness. So Mary has everything to learn, and has, so to speak, to find herself. She has not an easy time of it. She has to discover and face the worldliness of her father, his morality being rather different from that which she had learned in school, and at variance with that of the religion he is supposed to represent. He advises her to stand up for her rights and ever so gently suggests that she defy her husband if he deny her any of the social position the Dean had bargained for when he settled money and a house in town on the young couple. He advises: 'Men, and women too, ought to look after their own interests. It is the only way in which progress can be made in the world. Of course you are not to covet what belongs to others'—there speaks the clergymen, but the father adds, on the heels of this, 'you will make yourself very unhappy if you do' (xvi). It is a Baconian, a Franklinian morality: virtue is expedient. In the country, she is faced with the dull, humourless company of her husband, and the dreary good works of her sisters-in-law. No wonder that the season in the London house comes as a release, and that she finds pleasure in a certain Jack de Baron who happens to be available socially, and is everything witty and gay and amusing that her husband is not. She lives on the edge of an equivocal world where we do not know adultery as a fact, but we know it is considered as a possible course of action (xv, xx, xxix). Mary is far too good to do real wrong, but she is indiscreet with de Baron, and engages in a rather scandalous dance at an important ball; this is enough to make her vulnerable to vicious gossip, and to give grounds for what the Marquis so grossly exaggerates when he calls her a whore to her father's face, impugning the legitimacy of her expected child. So Mary must discover what freedoms are permissible and virtuous, precisely what constitutes 'flirting,' the social implications of waltzing; she must in fact make a study of virtue, all on her own, and its fine shades in specific cases. Trollope in an interesting chapter confronts her with certain pieces of advice she receives, both valid and yet quite at odds. 'She was the more perplexed, because both her instructors had appeared to her right in their teaching.' But we see her on the way to what Trollope calls 'a power, a certain intellectual alembic . . . by which she could distill the good of each, and quietly leave the residue behind her as being of no moment' (LXI and LXII). Here again is the Trollopian way of facing us with incongruities, and implying a moral result.

But before this, there has been a deal of trouble in the marriage. Lord George is not one to renounce the upper hand in marriage and Mary is anxious to test her rights and powers. Trollope more than once shows himself a fine anatomist of the marriage relationship. His most marvellous study of marriage is Palliser's and Lady Glencora's; but here too there is a beautifully drawn history of a power struggle between husband and wife, ploys and outploys, one-uppings, and vantages taken, all those activities recently studied by a psychologist as 'The Games People Play.' Here, in *Popenjoy*, Trollope observes that 'a husband's comfort is never perfect till some family peccadilloes have been conclusively proved against him. I am sure that a wife's temper to him is sweetened by such evidence of human imperfection' (XXXII). This though witty is also simply *true*. It is an ironic truth, that when Mary gains the vantage by catching George out in a little lapse, and then forgiving him, George profits by her increased tenderness to him.

In Mary's struggles to assert herself, a certain course is open to her: she could take up Women's Rights. London friends take her to a meeting of the 'Rights of Women Institute, Established for the Relief of the Disabilities of Females.' It is well known that Trollope has no friendship for the feminist movement; so one would think that here is an issue on which he does take sides. It seems to me, however, that even here he still maintains a detached and ironic attitude. No one who knows his picture of such women as Lady Laura Kennedy, whose obviously great ability is doomed to uselessness, can think he does not sympathise with women's frustrations. But then men's frustrations demand his sympathy too. He has an interesting way of turning the Woman Question back into a Human Question. In his lecture 'On the Higher Education of Women' he insists that there is no solution in feminism. What we *all* need, men and women, is 'a daily renewed resolution to do the best with ourselves within our power.' You young ladies, as the rest of mankind, need 'steadfast adherence to fixed purposes made by yourselves on your own behalf.'[1] The unfulfilled purpose of Sir Thomas Underwood in *Ralph the Heir* is as sad a failure as that of any woman. What Trollope consistently does is treat women as human beings primarily. All the virtues he understands by the word *manly* he will at times allow to women: Lady Jane Grey was *manly*, he says in hearty admiration.[2] This is a way of granting to women first-class citizenship in the human race; it may be a more humane course than taking sides for or against Rights. It is at least not simplistic. Women, he says, have always in all societies had certain inalienable rights. Even in Rome, *à propos* of Cicero's sister-in-law who was playing the martyr in that annoying way women have, he tells us that women 'have had the capacity to make themselves disagreeable in all ages.'[3]

Meantime, Mary Germain finds no solution to her own problems at the 'Disabilities,' as the Women's Rights Institute is disrespectfully called; for the feminists themselves are enough to put one off feminism. Their motives are, moreover, revealed as mercenary. Both speakers at the meeting are very terrible; and Trollope indulges himself in an obvious enough sort of humour about *la différence*. The Baroness Banmann, the formidable German architect, wears

. . . a cloth jacket buttoned up to the neck, which hardly gave to her copious bust that appearance of manly firmness which the occasion almost required. But the virile collars, budding out over it, perhaps supplied what was wanting.

The other speaker, Olivia Q. Fleabody, the Ph.D. from Vermont, 'was very thin, and the jacket and collars were quite successful' (xvii). I think what Trollope hates about feminism is the loss of femininity. He always cherishes identity, and sexual identity is a part of this. He begs his bright young American friend Kate Field not to proceed to the dried-up desexed stage, in pursuing her career, but to take herself a husband.[4] He holds up to her, and to Mary Germain, these horrors: the Baroness, Olivia Fleabody, and also Wallachia Petrie, 'the American Browning,' in *He Knew He Was Right*. In *Popenjoy*, a certain Mrs. Montacute Jones, who is a very knowing woman, advises our Mary: 'Women are quite able to hold their own without such trash as that!' (xxx.)

Irony dissipates the issue. Women who try to abrogate rights and powers are unaware that they have them if they care to exercise them. Mary makes her own solution to the Woman Question by defining her moral self in her particular social context. And the plaguey question of social class is also dissipated by ironies. When in due course the real true little English Popenjoy is born, an old female retainer is in an ecstasy of title-worship: 'Little angel! I know he'll grow up to bring new honours to the family, and do as much for it as his great grandfather.' The relentless Trollope comments, 'The great grandfather spoken of had been an earl, great in borough-mongery, and had been made a marquis by Pitt on the score of his votes' (lxiii). The Dean, whom we love for his attack on the marquis, is the better man.

But he had been subject to one weakness, which had marred a manliness which would otherwise have been great. He, who should have been proud of the lowliness of his birth, and have known that the brightest feather in his cap was the fact that, having been humbly born, he had made himself what he was, he had never ceased to be ashamed of the stableyard.

And he felt 'the only whitewash . . . was to be found in the aggrandisement of his daughter and the nobility of her children. He had, perhaps, been happier than he deserved' (LXIII). Lord George, that is, is luckily a good man and a good husband.

So in *Popenjoy* questions of propriety and class and sex are all bound up together. The fact that the Marquis has lived abroad draws some of our attention to English insularity *qua* insularity. When our good Lord George calls on his elder brother the Marquis and meets the Italian 'Marchioness,'

> It must have been a comfort to both of them that they spoke no common language, as they could hardly have had many thoughts to interchange with each other.
> 'I wonder why the deuce you never learned Italian,' said the Marquis.
> 'We never were taught,' said Lord George.
> 'No; nobody in England ever is taught anything but Latin and Greek—with this singular result, that after ten or a dozen years of learning not one in twenty knows a word of either language. That is our English idea of education. . . . My wonder is that Englishmen can hold their own in the world at all.'
> 'They do,' said Lord George, to whom all of this was ear-piercing blasphemy. . . .
> 'Yes; there is a ludicrous strength even in their pigheaded-ness. But I always think that Frenchmen, Italians and Prussians must, in dealing with us, be filled with infinite disgust. They must ever be saying "Pig, pig, pig," beneath their breath, at every turn.'
> 'They don't dare to say it out loud,' said Lord George.
> 'They are too courteous, my dear fellow' (XXXVI).

Again, Trollope is refining the over-simplification. The evil Marquis's splenetic criticism of English complacency has a certain intelligent wit that might give one pause:

'Your London doctors are such conceited asses. . . . Because they can make more money than their brethren in other countries they think that they know everything, and that nobody else knows anything. It is just the same with the English in every branch of life. The Archbishop of Canterbury is the greatest priest going, because he has the greatest income, and the Lord Chancellor the greatest lawyer. All you fellows here are flunkeys from top to bottom' (XLVIII).

The inarticulate Lord George is at a loss for defence, though he *knows* the Marquis wrong. Such passages incline us towards a detached view of the main matter of the novel.

Many of Trollope's stories of courtship, too, mix sex with political and social themes. In *The Belton Estate*, Clara Amedroz is torn between two lovers, one approved by all society and her friends as superior in station, and one who, though her own cousin, has sunk to the level of a mere farmer. But the approved lover, Captain Aylmer, M.P., shilly-shallies in the courtship, and it is finally as though Clara senses in him a sexual lack. I think the man is frigid or impotent. She at last follows her own good sense to accept the farmer cousin, Will Belton, whose virtue is matched by his positive sexuality. Very often in Trollope moral equivocation is linked with sexual equivocation; the three Stanhope children in *Barchester Towers*, for instance, are what he calls 'heartless' in spite of all their cleverness—incapable of warmth and incapable of virtue alike. Here in *The Belton Estate* the turning point is Will's passionate impulsive embrace of Clara, which utterly astounds her.

How was she to resent such passionate love? . . . Why—why—why! Why indeed;—except that it was needful for him that she should know the depth of his passion. . . . But before he went she told him that she had forgiven him, and she had preached to him a solemn, sweet sermon on the wickedness of yielding to momentary impulses. . . . but I think she loved him better when her sermon was finished than she had ever loved him before (XXII).

This is pretty tepid stuff to *our* ears, but the message is clear. Here, as generally, Trollope will not beg the question of 'the right true end of love.' He defends the love-making in his novels when he defends *Framley Parsonage*: 'It was downright honest love, in which there was no pretence on the part of the lady that she was too ethereal to be fond of a man. . . . Each of them longed for the other, and they were not ashamed to say so.'[5] He does not have to be clinical about sex; he just tells what he may of his character's sexual behaviour, and we know enough of their psychologies to read the rest. It is interesting that although living in a time of simpering ethereal females, Trollope's women have reminded more than one critic of Shakespeare's women. There is indeed often a heartiness and downrightness about them that is hardly to be outdone. Trollope knows what he is about in this, too. His Mary Lowther, in *The Vicar of Bullhampton*, he tells us, had Rosalind for her favourite heroine, 'because from the first moment of her passion she knew herself and what she was about, and loved her lover right heartily. Of all girls in prose or poetry she declared that Rosalind was the least of a flirt' (VIII). To Trollope, sexuality is valid, and so are the conventions of society, and he never loses interest in how the one must adjust to the other, and neither be denied.

Man's need for money and security is another fact of life, and how this too must be adjusted to the shifting conventions of society, and adjusted on terms that are moral, is the subject of one of Trollope's most important works, *The Way We Live Now*. The particular stress that is changing the conventions involved here is the new power of money. These were the days of the robber barons in the United States, and England too had its large-scale financiers.[6] Commercial enterprises were undertaken on a hitherto undreamed of scale, and laws had not yet had time to catch up with and control the new possibilities for financial chicanery. Nor had there been time to evaluate in moral terms the new kinds of financial practice. So there did indeed seem to be a threat of anarchy here, and many thoughtful men must have feared with Trollope that a new social hierarchy based on money alone threatened to replace the old social hierarchy based on 'blood' and land. The Old was not all good, but the threatening New was infinitely worse, so much worse that in this book Trollope is more urgent and less detached than in any of his others.

And yet I do not think it differs from the rest of his work as much as some critics claim. I have an idea that the title is an echo of Cicero's *Sic Vivitur,* and that Cicero's tone is Trollope's here, too. Cicero's occasion is a letter where he is half excusing, half apologising for indulging in flattery to serve a political end. He has flattered the powerful Appius, and comments wryly, *'Sed quid agas? Sic vivitur!'* Trollope's own translation runs: 'What would you have me do? It is thus we live now!'[7] There is social criticism in Cicero's words, and some self-criticism too, and there is a sadness that the old Republic has come to such a pass. But it is turned off in the form of ironic wit; the criticism is under fine emotional control. I think this is the case too with Trollope's *Way We Live Now.* This is how it is, he says: money is so powerful now, we can buy honesty all along the line—in literary circles, in politics, in society. 'What would you have us do? *Sic vivitur!'* By ironically pretending to accept the new *mores* he draws attention to what is evil in them. So, although in this book his purpose is more urgent than usual, his method is the same ironic *jeu d'esprit.*

Even here, he creates characters so real that we can understand them and therefore are obliged to extend to them at least a degree of sympathy. Even with the worst of them, the crooked financier Melmotte, we can at last, when he is broken and exposed, see into his murky self-awareness and appreciate a certain *virtù* in him. The next worst, young Felix Carbury, reaches his awful degradation by default really, not by overt crime, and one at last may well pity him as a somehow irretrievably lost soul. But for a bitter satire such as this novel is said to be, there is a great deal of good humour asserting itself. Take Adolphus ('Dolly') Longstaffe. He is idle and foolish and addicted to gambling, and there is a lot of Bertie Wooster about him that is delightfully funny. But then he comes to take on depth, and we see him in the round, and the funniness gets even funnier as he moves away from caricature. Coming out of an indifferent-to-vicious household, and consorting with the aimless and vicious young men of the Beargarden Club, it is all the more remarkable that he does have some principles of a sort, some elements of the 'gentleman.' He really does hate being told of the cheating at the club. The principle that he asserts when he says, 'If there is to be a row about cards, let it be in the card-room,' is not much of a principle, but it is something (xlix). He does truly object to his sister visiting at the house of Melmotte, and this scruple drives him to the most unwonted activity: he actually behaves as though she were alive and goes to see her and reprove her. Another instance of devotion occurs when she at last is to be married, and he sanctions the marriage with a gift chosen by himself, 'an enormous china dog, about five feet high' (xcv). This china dog is very ridiculous, and at the same time it has a moral sweetness about it that might bring an ambiguous tear to the eye.

It is not only the title and tone of the book that seems Ciceronian; the moral centre of the book seems to be presented specifically in Cicero's terms. The basis of the *De Officiis* is the differentiation of *honestum* and *turpe*, and I think this novel is Trollope's richest and most elaborate study of the Ciceronian differentiation. The most definitive study is his *Cousin Henry*, I think. In *Cousin Henry* he takes a single, unelaborated case to define the distinction; the case is isolated as though in that experimental manner we considered above, the better to examine the phenomenon in its purity. In brief: Henry Jones has inherited his uncle's fortune and takes possession of house and property. In the house he happens to discover a will, post-dating the one by which he inherits, which would make another cousin the heir. He is not an evil enough man to destroy this will, which he could have done

very easily without any threat of detection. But he lacks the
moral courage to make the virtuous action of reporting it, and
he leaves it hidden in the library where he found it. His
misery is acute as he lingers in a kind of moral limbo that
seems the very definition of Ciceronian turpitude.[8] It is to be
noted that when he is at last found out, he can be proved
guilty of no crime, legally, just as he is guilty of no overt
positive sin, morally. 'Not to do that which justice demands
is so much easier to the conscience than to commit a deed
which is palpably fraudulent!' (xxiii.) The sin is one of
omission; he has failed in courage to take the positive action
honestum requires. And it would seem that the failure to take
the right action, the 'leaving undone those things which we
ought to have done,' is just about as base as overt crime.
Certainly it desecrates the ideal of 'manliness' or *honestum*.
Virtue, *honestum*, demands more than inaction, more than the
avoidance of crime.

The Way We Live Now elaborates this concept. In Cicero's
day the threat was Caesarism—might makes right—and
Cicero laboured incessantly, Trollope is at pains to show, to
take action against it.[9] Now, in Trollope's day, the threat is
that money makes might makes right. And Trollope is at
pains to show that passivity is silent acquiescence, and
amounts to condoning the evil and therefore is virtually as
evil as the financial dishonesty itself. It is very slight derelictions of duty, derelictions that might in some contexts even
seem virtuous, that in effect add up to a great social evil.
Even in the election when Melmotte campaigns for the seat
of Westminster, his supporters, Trollope says, are honest and
good men. They have believed the principles Melmotte
declares, which he does not at all believe in himself. It is easy
and convenient to believe in him. Both the Roman Catholic
Father Barham and the Anglican Bishop accept, for their
churches, his charity, without much scruple as to the motivation (lv). In a sense, he buys their support, although both are
highly virtuous men, putting cause well before any selfish

interest. The new finance offers such possibilities to the right causes that its probity in itself is not looked to.

The new finance creates a sort of snobbery too: one must pretend to understand. Finance is part of the masculine mystique. And so the splendid comedy, and sad hypocrisy, of the great Board of the South Central Pacific and Mexican Railway, consists in this: that not one member (except Melmotte and his aide) understands what a Board is or what he is doing on it, and yet all are too proud to confess to ignorance, for a long time. The lot of them—the two Grendalls, Lord Nidderdale, Paul Montague, and Dolly Longstaffe—are of course being used as a respectable front for a nefarious operation. The Board continues to function in its fog-bound way till at last it is Dolly Longstaffe, the simplest-minded one, who with all his sins has a certain modesty, and the honesty or naïveté to say at last, 'I don't comprehend these things' (LVIII). And through a simple desire to get back the 'tin' he has been cozened of, he is the one to discover the swindle, in a sort of Emperor's-new-clothes situation.

The Railway Board is one of those situations that bring together many elements in ironic interplay. The greatest focal situation in the novel, that brings in the whole range, is the state dinner that Melmotte gives for the visiting Emperor of China. Here, Trollope makes his serious moral points with a special abundance of humour. Trollope is always good at guest lists, or seating arrangements at dinner parties,[10] because they involve fine shades in social relationships; and this great dinner for the Emperor has a guest list to end them all. Two hundred of the greatest in England are to be chosen for the dinner, and eight hundred of the next-to-greatest are to come in after dinner. Royalty, peers and peeresses, ambassadors and such like constitute the two hundred; then there are to be 'three wise men, two poets, three independent members of the House of Commons, two Royal Academicians, three editors of papers, an African traveller who had just come home, and a novelist.' All these latter are in the second class of the two hundred, as they are to come only as bachelors; they receive no tickets for their wives. Adjustments are continually being made. A certain writer must be included: 'Was it because he had praised the Prime Minister's translation of Catullus?' (xxxv.) And then:

> A novelist was selected; but as royalty wanted another ticket at the last moment, the gentleman was only asked to come in after dinner. His proud heart, however, resented the treatment, and he joined amicably with his literary brethren in decrying the festival altogether (xxxv).

It would not seem from all this that Trollope has lost any of his artistic ironic detachment. The incident of the novelist is one of those 'intrusions' where the author reminds us of himself, and thereby amuses us while he takes the artistic advantage of reinforcing the ironic relationship. The brotherhood of novelists withhold their approval, not from moral principle but from hurt pride. *Così fan tutte.*

All the jockeying for place is a humourous drama in little of the vanity of human motivations. This swindler who succeeds only because he is superior in swindling infects society because society turns Cousin Henry. It knows, but it will not take the virtuous action necessary. It is so easy to do as everyone else does. To join in the struggle for a ticket is tantamount to condoning the morals of a man everyone has good reason to doubt. 'It does sometimes occur in life that an unambitious man, who is in no degree given to enterprises, who would fain be safe, is driven by the cruelty of circumstances into a position in which he must choose a side' (LIX). Trollope puts his characters into these 'cruel circumstances,' which are, to be brief, the usual circumstances of human life. *Honestum* demands more than non-crime; it demands positive virtuous action. Another one of those recurrent Latin tags Trollope finds frequent occasion for is *descensus averni*; the easy way is the way to hell. Felix Carbury's crime is mostly inaction; Lady Carbury's is just doing as they all do—in her case in order to get money for her spoiled son; men go to

Melmotte's dinner because everyone else does. 'What follows as a natural consequence? Men reconcile themselves to swindling. Though they themselves mean to be honest, dishonesty of itself is no longer odious to them' (LV). *Sic vivitur.*

But this 'dark' book is nevertheless a melioristic one. It is the character Roger Carbury not the author Anthony Trollope who voices the spleen of the century. The view of the Anglican Bishop is set against Roger's; for unlike Roger, the Bishop 'was not hopelessly in love . . . and was therefore less inclined to take a melancholy view of things in general than Roger Carbury. To Roger everything seemed to be out of joint.' The Bishop takes a longer view:

> '. . . they who grumble at the times, as Horace did, and declare that each age is worse than its forerunner, look only at the small things beneath their eyes, and ignore the course of the world at large.'
>
> 'But Roman freedom and Roman manners were going to the dogs when Horace wrote.'
>
> 'But Christ was about to be born . . .' answers the Bishop.

And more specifically:

> 'It is very hard to see into the minds of men, but we can see the results of their minds' work. I think that men on the whole do live better lives than they did a hundred years ago. There is a wider spirit of justice abroad, more of mercy from one to another, a more lively charity, and if less of religious enthusiasm, less also of superstition. Men will hardly go to heaven, Mr. Carbury, by following forms only because their fathers followed the same forms before them' (LV).

And he predicts that Melmotte—the spectacle of whose success is so profoundly depressing to Roger—will be exposed. And this indeed happens. When he takes his seat as Member for Westminster his bankruptcy both moral and economic becomes apparent, and Melmotte's occupation's gone, and in dark solitude he swallows prussic acid.

The Bishop's view is 'in character,' and is only that of a 'character,' and therefore we cannot take it as Trollope's.

Indeed it is Roger Carbury who *sounds* most like Trollope himself in this book, and this is why the book is generally considered so bitter. Nevertheless the Bishop's words oblige us to correlate the *inside* perspectives with the *outside*, more detached one; and suggest that it is possible to invent new 'forms' more answerable to the changed times. We cannot put the Bishop out of the novel; he presents that double perspective Trollope always insists on, whereby he imposes a new still wider, wiser vantage-point.

*   *   *

The American Senator is perhaps the supreme instance of Trollope's multi-perspective method: the Senator is himself the highly objective correlative of the comparativistic attitude, and the internationalism of the subject gives this novel a wide range. The Senator as a device is reminiscent of a classical critical mode: the *locus classicus* is Montesquieu's *Lettres persanes*. Montesquieu takes his foreigner, a Persian, puts him down in the middle of the French culture which his readers know from the inside, and sets him to writing letters home that record his impressions of that culture. By juxtaposing this new view with our ordinary inside informed view of things, Montesquieu establishes yet a new perspective that takes both the others into account and brings with it a new understanding of human society. It works like this: The Persian writes his observations of what goes on around him, and we are enormously amused at his misunderstanding and naïveté. Then as we laugh, we cannot help wondering how he came to get such impressions, and then we may realise he has discovered something of the truth that has escaped us. By this manipulation of perspectives, Montesquieu is able to comment on society with a humour and candour that are quite distinctive. The reader has the delight of the discovery, and at the same time is led away from monisms and prejudices up into an area of detached comparativism; up away from the trees, so he can see at last, the woods. How illuminating and enfranchising this can be, everybody knows. The trees will perhaps never look quite the same once we have seen the woods. It becomes possible to see the relativity of religions, governments, manners and philosophies. *'Verité dans un temps, erreur dans un autre'* (Lettre LXXV). Goldsmith does the same thing when he sets up his Chinese observer in London, and his aim is made clear by his title 'Citizen of the World.' He would enlarge us from our insularity, and let us see ourselves from a more detached and more informed perspective.

The American Senator is Trollope's Citizen of the World. The prototypes, both the Persian and the Chinese, are fictions that quickly become transparent, and we soon realise the game the author is up to. But the Senator, because he is in a Trollopian novel, does not become transparent at all. He is solid republican meat, and he becomes progressively more solid through the novel. He starts as a grotesque, the absurdly naïve Yankee abroad, and then takes on more and more human dimensions. The realistic mode disguises the conventional device, and ultimately enriches it too. The Senator comes from the great western American State of Mickewa, on leave from his legislative duties to study the English in their natural habitat. His interests are broad-ranging, and he writes to his friend back home in Washington to record his discoveries. Through his friend John Morton, whom he had known in the British Embassy in Washington, he has entrée into various circles in London and in the country. He falls to with a will, pokes here and there, and comments with a most praiseworthy, if annoying, honesty. He is interested in everything, and quickly thinks he understands everything. But, of course, *we* see how he misunderstands almost everything, and makes a fool of himself for his amused English friends. The funniest thing of all, however, is that this absurd American is invariably dead right in his criticism of things English. We become progressively more and more convinced of the Senator's good faith and his moral intelligence. We come to sympathise with him in his frustrations, as he realises the cold light of his reasonableness will not succeed in convincing the English of their malpractices, but only annoys and offends them.

The Senator in his interplay with the English is much more than Montesquieu's Persian. He is involved with the English; and still more important, we are involved with him. While he teaches us to evaluate our English selves, the Englishmen's reactions to the Senator teach us to evaluate our American selves, and so consequently there is a delightfully complicated counter-play going on, all about international relations. Trollope always feels rather responsible about American friendship. His mother's *Domestic Manners* did a great deal for the Trollope family finances but not much for international relations. He confesses to a hope that he might redress some of the ill will his mother's book had occasioned.[11] In his *North America* he is perpetually striving to be conscientious in observation and impartial in evaluation. More than once, he declares the value of the larger view, and proclaims a sort of internationalism.

> As a rule patriotism is a virtue only because man's aptitude for good is so finite, that he cannot see and comprehend a wider humanity.[12]
> There is much that is higher and better and greater than one's country. One is patriotic only because one is too small and too weak to be cosmopolitan.[13]

He is especially aware of the difficulties that beset Anglo-American relations, and he shows they are his concern in this particular novel.

> When an intelligent Japanese travels in Great Britain or an intelligent Briton in Japan, he is struck with no wonder at national differences. He is on the other hand rather startled to find how like his strange brother is to him in many things. Crime is persecuted, wickedness is condoned, and goodness treated with indifference in both countries. Men care more for what they eat than anything else, and combine a closely

defined idea of meum with a lax perception as to tuum. Barring a little difference of complexion and feature the Englishman would make a good Japanese, or the Japanese a first-class Englishman. But when an American comes to us or a Briton goes to the States, each speaking the same language, using the same cookery, governed by the same laws, and wearing the same costume, the differences which present themselves are so striking that neither can live six months in the country of the other without a holding up of hands and a torrent of exclamations. And in nineteen cases out of twenty the surprise and the ejaculations take the place of censure. The intelligence of the American, displayed through the nose, worries the Englishman. The unconscious self-assurance of the Englishman, not always unaccompanied by a sneer, irritates the American (LXXVII).

The two countries are, as some other wit has said, separated by the barrier of a common language. However much the specific issues have shifted in focus, the barrier still exists in our century, as anyone who has ever lived in both countries knows. Where we expect to understand we are baffled and irritated. The counterplay of the novel is so delightfully managed that neither English nor American reader can take offence and both are absolutely forced by laughter into tolerance. The Senator's moral logic is juxtaposed with the condoning circumstances the reader knows in all their complications. Trollope himself writes in a letter that he does not think the Senator's character will offend American readers, for he is 'a thoroughly honest man wishing to do good, and is not himself so absurd as the things which he criticises.'[14] One critic thinks he used the title *The American Senator* to increase his American sales.[15] This may be so. We do know he stuck to it in spite of his publisher's advice.[16] I believe he wanted this title because it would remind the reader of the outside, ironic view of things even when he is following the story lines which the Senator personally plays little part in.

It is the view his art is always invoking: the insistence on the two incongruities in *The Warden* case itself enforces it.

This art tends naturally to the device of the foreign observer. Even when he is not writing a story, Trollope is trying to achieve the outside, detached assessment. For instance, in *The Clergymen of the Church of England,* he describes how bishops are chosen:

> How English, how absurd, how picturesque it all is!—and, we may add, how traditionally useful! The Queen is the head of the Church, and therefore sends down word to a chapter, which in truth as a chapter no longer exists, that it has permission to choose its bishop, the bishop having been already appointed by the Prime Minister, who is the nominee of the House of Commons! The chapter makes its choice accordingly, and the whole thing goes on as though the machine were kept in motion by forces as obedient to reason and the laws of nature as those operating on a steam-engine. We are often led to express our dismay, and sometimes our scorn, at the ignorance shown by foreigners as to our institutions; but when we ourselves consider their complications and ir-rationalistic modes of procedure, the wonder is that any one not to the manner born should be able to fathom aught of their significance.[17]

It is only by trying to act the foreigner that we can evaluate our institutions. Our human institutions may seem to compound the un-reason of individual human beings, in their absurdity. And yet if the institutions have survived it is because they work just as if by rational means. And if they work, we had better respect them. For however English, absurd, or picturesque they are, they seem to be also 'traditionally useful.'

America is the child of the Age of Reason, Trollope would say, and has in fact been able to establish things on a basis more rational than the old, and its representative, the Senator, is the best type of this new rational being because he is so honest and so concerned for justice. And he is not stupid, either, only somewhat too inclined to expect pure rationality from the human race. Trollope suggests by his title that we watch the Arabella Trefoil–Morton–Rufford story two ways: as the

Senator might see it, and as we know it to be, in all its involvement and subtlety and complication. Then we can better understand and evaluate. The same holds true of the Mary Masters–Morton–Twentyman plot. Both these stories *have* to be long, because Trollope has to give us an understanding of the involved and subtle complications of each, in order to point the contrast with the Senator's shallow simplifications. Both the Arabella story and the Mary story are love triangles, involving interplay on classes, and morals of courtship; the two make nice contrast in themselves. And we, with the Senator at the back of our minds, or on the cover of the book whenever we pick it up, remember the double view: the superficial, rationalistic one, and the deep, detailed, circumstantial one and we are obliged to make some correlation. Both views seem 'true.'

The plot the Senator plays a part in is significant in itself. It is the story of the friends and enemies of the sport of hunting, and it is a good subject to involve the Senator in, because devotion to sport is a phase of human behaviour that is least defensible on logical grounds. Trollope tells us in the *Autobiography* of the days in Ireland when he took up hunting, and 'then and there began one of the great joys of my life. I have ever since been constant to the sport, having learned to love it with an affection which I cannot myself fathom or understand.'[18] The Senator is too much the rationalist ever to enjoy something he could not think he understood; and Trollope is too much the empiricist to deny the existence of his joy or his sure sense of its beneficence. But he very well knows the absurd aspects of hunting.

Just as the Senator comes to appraise the whole phenomenon, the country is rocked by the terrible Goarly case. Goarly is a scoundrel of a farmer whose crops have been slightly damaged by the hunt, and the rascally goose who constitutes Mrs. Goarly's ill-conducted poultry yard has had a nasty scare. Goarly goes so far in his revenge as to lay out poison for the foxes, and the very first hunt the Senator sees begins with the horrifying discovery of a poisoned fox. The hounds are quickly shut into Larry Twentyman's barn to be safe from the poison, and the fox is laid on a little bier while the dumb-struck huntsmen gather round to look. 'The men around gazed into each other's faces with a sad tragic air. . . . The dreadful word "vulpecide" was heard from various lips with an oath or two before it' (x). This foolish little term, of course, insists on one way of looking at hunting, and discovers to us how the hunter's own torture and killing of the fox is not considered *vulpecide* at all, though it must be more dreadful to the fox. To the Senator it all seems too silly for words, and he has difficulty in keeping a serious air in his investigations.

One aspect of the case catches his serious republican eye, however. Goarly's grain has been trampled by Lord Rufford and his hunting friends; and the Senator seizes on this as a case of the down-trodden serf trying to survive while the cruel landlord destroys his means of livelihood. *We* know the delicate ecological balance a hunting county requires: foxes, pheasants, woods, and occasional sacrifice of some small part of a crop and some barnyard fowls. The tenant is generally overcompensated in money for whatever loss he has; on Lord Rufford's estate, very much so. But the Senator takes up Goarly's case, even indiscreetly contributing money to Goarly's lawyer. By degrees he discovers how he has been cozened, how Goarly is a blackguard and a double dealer. But he still at the end complains that his English friends fail to see that even if this particular serf is a scoundrel, the principle is still wrong. There should be no overlord who has the right to overrun his tenant's crop. The situation parallels that of *The Warden*: the instrument of the old abuse is Lord Rufford, kindly, just and beneficent, like Mr. Harding; the victim of the abuse is Goarly, even farther from virtue than the greedy old• men of Hiram's Hospital; the righteous reformer is the Senator, like John Bold in devotion to logic and principle. Goarly is a blackguard, the Senator finds out, but he insists a blackguard may have a good cause (LXVIII).

179

The most terrible abuses that the Senator finds are the abuses of representative government. He goes to the town of Quinborough to see how an election works:

> Quinborough was a little town of 3,000 inhabitants clustering round the gates of a great Whig Marquis, which had been spared,—who can say why?—at the first Reform Bill, and having but one member had come out scatheless from the second. Quinborough still returned its one member with something less than 500 constituents, and in spite of household suffrage and the ballot had always returned the member favoured by the Marquis. This nobleman, driven no doubt by his conscience to make some return to the country for the favour shown to his family, had always sent to Parliament some useful and distinguished man who without such patronage might have been unable to serve his country. On the present occasion a friend of the people,—so called,—an unlettered demagogue such as is in England in truth distasteful to all classes, had taken himself down to Quinborough as a candidate in opposition to the nobleman's nominee. He had been backed by all the sympathies of the American Senator who new nothing of him or his unfitness, and nothing whatever of the patriotism of the Marquis. But he did know what was the population and what the constituency of Liverpool, and also what were those of Quinborough. He supposed that he knew what was the theory of representation in England, and he understood correctly that hitherto the member for Quinborough had been the nominee of that great lord. These things were horrid to him. There was to his thinking a fiction, —more than fiction, a falseness,—about all this which not only would but ought to bring the country prostrate to the dust. When the working-man's candidate, whose political programme consisted of a general disbelief in all religions, received—by ballot!—only nine votes from those 500 voters, the Senator declared to himself that the country must be rotten to the core. It was not only that Britons were slaves,— but that they 'hugged their chains' (LI).

This Quinborough election is a miniature of the Trollopian novel-situation.

We see him exposed to a variety of abuses and anomalies. At the dinner party of the charming and worldly rector, Mr.

Mainwaring, whose living had been bought for him with his
wife's money, there is a wealth of comic dramatic irony, as
the Senator asks his bland questions about the ways of church
preferment. It is hardly fair that a clergyman who profits by
such abuse should nevertheless be beneficent in his office.
And then there is the further rich irony of the letters the
Senator writes to his friend in Washington, to whom he can
be more frank, and we profit by more of his outside view. He
grants the English much: the charm and sweetness of their
manners, which make him think of himself as Ulysses among
the Lotus-eaters; and he sees their moral values, their desire
to live up to principles, though he thinks the principles are
bad. But Lord Rufford, in spite of his grace, is, in fact, idle,
ignorant, and self-satisfied. (The criticism here reminds one of
Arnold on the Barbarians.) There is a pretty good tolerance
of free speech, he finds. But he finds the rich are 'nicer' than
the poor, just because the poor are so abject and grovelling,
and refuse to resent their position. In Parliament, he finds
grandeur in everything, but no eloquence. It is all very
glorious but reminds the Senator of 'a last year's nut, of which
the outside appearance has been mellowed and improved by
time—but the fruit inside has withered away and become
tasteless' (LI). He visits Lord Rufford's 'model farm' and is
shocked to find it is a toy, not a useful example to anyone.
Here he sounds like Trollope himself as he brings in that
eternal shoemaker who always serves as the example of honest
work for a living (LXVIII).

Of the three plots, then, the Senator plot takes its structure
from that basic Trollopian unit of the Warden-situation, and
this Senator plot, the slightest of the three, makes a framework for the whole, culminating in his grand lecture to the
English Public on the irrationality of the English—which
whole subject develops consistently out of his reaction to the
Goarly case. The English see Goarly's evil, and the Senator
sees the Rational Principle. The other plots are love stories,
and overlap very little with the Senator's, but Trollope's love

stories often have wide social and political significance, and we can consider these two in relation to the Senator's theme.

The love story of Mary Masters depends in large part on delicate gradations in class structure and the effect they have on Mary's rejection of Larry Twentyman and her acceptance of Reginald Morton. If anyone had tried to explain it to the Senator, he would have snapped his fingers at it. And yet we know these delicate gradations make agony for Mary, and not in any way so simple as just that she wants to marry higher in the scale rather than lower. Larry Twentyman is a good, hearty, faithful man, with a financial competence, too, and Mary knows it and loves him—but not as a lover. There are matters of sheer intelligence and sensitivity, qualities fostered in Mary by her protectress, Lady Ushant; and these qualities occur more often in the leisured well-read gentle class than in the farmer stock of Larry, no matter how good. And there is a little swagger in Larry that is in itself not gentle; and when in the grief of his rejected love the swagger falters, he is even less a man. Mary's stepmother, who persecutes her for rejecting Larry, is in herself a vivid demonstration of just how offensive a certain lower-middle-classishness of outlook can be. Reginald Morton, the gentleman lover, on the other hand, is, we know, rather bookish, and as opportunities arise in the story we discover he is not as staid as we thought, but has a little gift for wit. And when things turn out well for him and Mary accepts him, his sallies positively sparkle. Larry at last finds himself and very happily marries Mary's half-sister Kate, a hearty, horsey girl, who is lower in the social scale.

The hunting combines classes in an interesting way. That irrational joy of being alive that is proper to it is something of a leveller. I have said Trollope is not a propagandist, but now must qualify that: he is downrightly, uncompromisingly and consistently against charity bazaars (*Miss Mackenzie*, xxvii), and he is even more downrightly, uncompromisingly and consistently in favour of hunting. So Reginald Morton steps a little out of character here to defend it. Although a bookish man, he declares he will take up hunting just to give it his blessing, in the face of the 'philanimalists,' the self-styled 'philosophers,' who 'not looking very clearly into the systems of pains and pleasures in accordance with which we have to live . . . call upon the world to curse the cruelty of those who will not agree with them' (LXXIII). The activity that appears so idiotic to the Senator is in fact a blessing to our irrational existential selves.

The story of Arabella Trefoil and her pursuit of Lord Rufford makes a sharp contrast with the story of Mary, who plays a waiting game and wins. Mary's position in the social hierarchy is ambivalent, but her taste in behaviour is perfect; Arabella, although niece of a Duke, functions on a law-of-the-jungle ethic. The Senator has had some opportunity to observe Arabella in action, and his misunderstanding is monumental. At the terrible last crisis when she comes and does her Medean worst to Lord Rufford, leaving the party at the Hall shaken, as she retreats on foot to the lodge, the Senator is about to sit down to lunch with the Lord and his protective she-dragons who have been horrified to see him almost caught by Arabella. The Senator glimpses her going off, and 'with his marvellous gift of saying awkward things' has no idea that the occasion calls for reticence. He remarks: 'Miss Trefoil always gave me the idea of being a good type of English aristocracy.' We know her as its saddest product, the women think she is something like a devil, and to Lord Rufford she has lately been a scourge (LXVIII).

The Senator's bland ignorance contrasts with our well-developed understanding. Arabella is frigid, calculating, cruel, selfish, hunts for men only for position and money, and throws a good man over if a richer is in sight. Victorian women are supposed to faint often, but they don't much in Trollope. Arabella's fainting is fake. It occurs when she has Rufford in a compromising position, in the hired carriage on the way home from the hunt. She is exhausted, and in his arms, and it is easy enough to close her eyes, and yet she is never more calculating. 'As she thought of it all she affected to swoon, and almost herself believed that she was swooning. She was conscious but hardly more than conscious that he was kissing her;—and yet her brain was at work' (xxxix). She has almost no scruples. Early in her pursuit of Rufford, when she is playing hard, staking everything on only a few days' stay at Rufford Hall, there is a hunting accident which she is able to turn to good use, a terrible and as it turns out mortal accident, which she has the good luck to witness closely with Rufford near her. She is able to lean on him in her state of shock, and she makes good capital later of this shared experience: it is something to bring them close in conversation and creates an intimacy, and later something to need to write letters about. Poor Major Caneback's death is invaluable to her.

The ironic use of Caneback is very Trollopian, a rich and ambivalent thing, anyway. He is a man none of them cares for in the least; he 'earned hospitality by his prowess as a horse-tamer. He did this once too often, for the mare Jemima kicked him on the skull, and he died as he had lived, almost without speech' (xxvi). But poor blank sort of man that he is, he creates a great social problem with his accident. There is to be a ball that night, and should it be called off?

> A ball, with a dead man in one of the bedrooms, would be dreadful. With a dying man it was bad enough. . . ! Had the major been dying three or four miles off, at the hotel at Rufford, there would have been a few sad looks, a few shakings of the head, and the people would have danced without any flaw in their gaiety. . . . He was not a man worthy of much care. He was possessed of infinite pluck, and now that he was dying could bear it well. . . . But nevertheless it is a bore when a gentleman dies in your house (xxiii).

It is one of Trollope's moral dilemmas, concerned with delicate degrees of feeling that must dictate behaviour. Need the ball be called off if the death is expected by the local doctor?

Or may it go on if the London surgeon expects recovery? Or, if there is a ball, should it be modified? And if so, how much? It is Trollope's relentless way to test principles in these difficult cases, and he wrings much rueful humour from this ambivalent death.

Arabella loses and gets an advantage. There is a compromise about the ball: it will go on, but be curtailed, and the ladies staying at the Hall will dance only a little, to start things off. So Arabella misses the opportunities much dancing might give her, but the lull gives her a chance to get Rufford off in a small room by himself and to entangle him in an embrace.

But our interest goes beyond the mere story of Arabella's hunt. Senator in mind, we look at her as a cultural phenomenon; and she is deplorable. She is obviously the product of a system. As dowerless girl and niece to a Duke, she has to take on the business of hunting down money and position; and the business-like-ness would seem to create the frigidity, which is really the cause of her just-missing so often. Her lovers back out, and she ages, and the whole business gets more dreary and wearisome every year, and she and her dreadful mother progress from frank calculation to foul recrimination and mutual hate. In the beautifully ironic scene where her uncle, aunt, father, and cousin meet to decide how to try to help her, they all, in spite of professed concern, back out and decide they will ask her mother to interview Rufford:

> All these influential members of the ducal family met together at the ducal mansion on Arabella's behalf, and settled their difficulty by deputing the work of bearding the lion, of tying the bell on the cat, to an absent lady whom they all despised and disliked (LX).

Her father cares only for his club and whist and wine, and yet he postures as outraged, 'as much as to say that his feelings as a British parent were almost too strong for him' (LX). He is no help to her whatsoever. The mere mention of

185

'British' shows the comparativistic idea at work here. All this suggests themes sometimes supposed to have been discovered by Henry James; but James was not, in fact, the first in the field.

The finale of the book is the occasion of the Senator's public oration on 'The Irrationality of Englishmen,' which is surely one of the grand pieces of comic writing of the age (LXXVII and LXVIII). Here is the Senator's survey of the whole of England, and a survey of the English reaction to that survey, and our survey of the incongruity of inside view and outside view, of the honesty on both sides, and of the great barriers. The Senator's good faith is never more evident than now; we must love him thoroughly. And yet he offends his hearers to the point of open public disturbance.

> He could not liberate his soul without doing something in public to convince his cousins that in their general practices of life they were not guided by reason. . . . It should not be his fault if the absurdities of a people whom he really loved were not exposed to light, so that they might be acknowledged and abandoned (LXXVII).

The Senator points out the unreason here, and here, and here. He will, he says, tell it all to his countrymen, as well as report all the good things he has found. But he cannot, he says, ever tell them of the practices of hunting, because he would not be believed. But now, for his English audience, he covers a lot—Parliament, suffrage, class system—while, irrationally, the irritation of his audience is rising to a somewhat threatening degree. There is a lull when the Senator points out abuses in the Church, for 'it is not often that the British public is angered by abuse of the Church.' On the matter of the Army, he is on more dangerous ground. He confesses a particular difficulty in understanding things here: 'Unhappily I have found it in a state of transition, and nothing is so difficult to a stranger's comprehension as a transition state of affairs'—a nice general implication, for it is one of Trollope's axioms that everything is always in a state

of transition. And the Senator's other comments on the
Army have, to us, a similarly general implication, on various
levels. In the Army, says the Senator, he can see,

> that every improvement which is made is received by those
> whom it most concerns with a horror which amounts almost
> to madness. So lovely to the ancient British, well-born,
> feudal instinct is a state of unreason, that the very absence
> of any principle endears it to institutions which no one can
> attempt to support by argument. . . . I say that the change
> [in the army] was forced upon you by the feeling of the people,
> but that its very expediency has demoralized the army,
> because the army was irrational.

We may remember and compare Walter Bagehot's irony: how
much of the success of political man depends on *stupidity*;
and how the strength of royalty is in its appeal to diffused
feelings, and the weakness of republics is in its appeal to
the understanding. So strong is the devotion to absurdities
in the Senator's English audience that at last the heckling
sounds dangerous and the lecture is discontinued. The Chair-
man, Lord Drummond, expresses his regrets to the Senator:
'I cannot tell you how much I respect both your purpose and
your courage;—but I don't know how far it is wise for a man
to tell any other man, much less a nation, of all his faults.'
'You English tell us of ours pretty often,' says the Senator
(LXXVIII).

The layers of irony here become even more complicated.
Although the Senator is a patient man and modest, he at last
feels angry, Trollope says. He feels angry 'because people
were unreasonable with him, which was surely unreasonable
in him, who accused Englishmen generally of want of reason.
One ought to take it as a matter of course that a bull should
use his horns, and a wolf his teeth' (LXXX). Poor Man, that
unreason must be his characteristic tool! The Senator gives us
a lecture on the irrationality of the English, while Trollope is
giving us a laughing lecture on the irrationality of Mankind.
The Senator goes home, and 'when we last heard of him was

187

thundering in the Senate against certain practices on the part of his own country which he thought to be unjust to other nations. Don Quixote was not more just than the Senator, or more philanthropic,—nor perhaps more apt to urge war against the windmills' (LXXX). These are Trollope's last words on the Senator, in the last chapter of the book. The mention of the Don at this point is a reminder of the grand comic tradition of the novel.

Furthermore, Trollope's use of the eighteenth-century device of the foreigner lends to the realistic line of the nine-teenth-century novel a classical kind of witty criticism. The device enables him to impose a large, relativistic view, and the realism makes the view dynamic. It is not a matter of just the Senator, or just an American in England. It is a matter of human being to human being. As we can see in instances of dramatic irony how men can misunderstand one another so we can imagine instances of a larger dramatic irony involving nations. Our justice and our philanthropy, so excellent and indispensable in principle, must be continually educated and adjusted to transition, which is the condition of life. And then they must be continually adjusted to the specific case. The Senator as *eiron* is a great technical success, but it is not uncharacteristic of Trollope. Although distinctive, it is only a more than usually specific objectivation of the attitude that marks his work: a zest for life, a relentless revelation of the human absurd, and an encompassing charity. Perhaps this novel affords him occasion to bring to our attention his widest panorama of social phenomena, and perhaps it has the widest perspective of all his works. In refusing exclusive loyalty to either nation, he declares his own passionate loyalty to the whole of the human race.

NOTES

[1]*Four Lectures*, ed. Morris L. Parrish, pp. 86, 88.

[2]*Cicero*, I, 298.

[3]II, 80.

[4]*Letters*, p. 261.

[5]*Autobiography*, p. 121.

[6]There is interesting background material for Trollope's Melmotte, and Dicken's Merdle, too, in the study of Hudson in *Enter Rumour*, by R. B. Martin. New York, W. W. Norton, 1962.

[7]Cicero, II, 114; *Ad. Div.*, says Trollope. We can find it *Ad. Fam.*, lib. ii, 15; Loeb, p. 138.

[8]The same problem, in the form of a moral dilemma, occurs in the *De Officiis*, III, xii; Loeb, p. 53. 'Aliud est celare, aliud tacere.' See my article, *NCF*, June, 1969, '*Cousin Henry:* Trollope's Note from Antiquity.'

[9]See below, where the Bishop and Carbury compare England to Rome.

[10]One good example of dinner-party seating is in Chapter XIII of *Popenjoy*. Trollope must have used algebra, or place cards arranged by trial and error, to make it work out as well as it does.

[11]See the Introduction to his *North America*, eds. Donald Smalley and Bradford A. Booth. New York, Alfred A. Knopf, 1951, pp. 3–4.

[12]*North America*, p. 89.

[13]*Letters*, ed. Bradford A. Booth. New York, 1951, pp. 178–179. There is an excellent study of this, 'Trollope's Cosmopolitanism,' *NCF*, II, June, 1947, 3–10.

[14]*Letters*, p. 357.

[15]David Stryker, 'The Significance of Trollope's *American Senator*,' *NCF*, V, September, 1950, 141–149.

[16]*Letters*, p. 347.

[17]*Clergymen of the Church of England*. London, 1866, p. 41.

[18]*An Autobiography*, ed. Bradford A. Booth, p. 53.

Chapter VIII

THE ANGEL OF LIGHT

'Do you think that I mean nothing because I laugh at myself?'

TROLLOPE, *Is He Popenjoy?*

TROLLOPE'S art may be best characterised as the art of the ironic perspective, and to appreciate it as such may open some insights into the art of the novel in general. *Irony*—the word challenges definition, applying as it does to so many things, from the slightest verbal sarcasm to the ultimate ontologies. Sometimes it equals Humour, sometimes Art, sometimes the view of God, so that one might feel it can never be precise enough to be useful. But the way the word is is the way we must use it, and even its very variety of meanings can serve to show something of the psyche itself: men have seen relevancies between irony as trope and irony in human life, and between both these and irony as a moral attitude. Its range suggests that for a certain discernible state of affairs there is a rhetoric that best suits, and an attitude of mind that best suits. The ironist objectifies a connection between ethics and art, a connection well demonstrated some time ago by the French psychologist Frédéric Paulhan, in *La Morale de l'ironie*. He declares all ethical precepts are like absentee landlords, 'préfets d'un gouvernement lointain'; and so are all 'virtues,' 'points of honour,' all special or systematic ethics.[1] The novel of casuistry, then, like Trollope's, is the objective correlative of the Ethics of Irony. The irony is in the style, of course, but more demonstrable in the structure of the content, the structure according to ambivalent case.

To say one thing and to mean another—that is the basic sense of the word *irony*, the one usually taken first. But in connection with ironic novels it is best to declare a subdivision here; *irony* is not like *allegory* in its doubleness. Allegory works by saying one thing *in terms of* another, but in irony the 'one thing' and the 'other' are contrasting facets of reality, and must be balanced and kept in mind together. When Coriolanus shouts in desperation that he will deal *gently*, we are aware of two things, chiefly: one, he intends to be gentle, and two, he cannot possibly be so. It is richly funny, and it is extraordinarily sad. To appreciate this ambivalence is to move further off and assume a new attitude that takes cognisance of the previous two. This new induced attitude is, I think, the typical process of irony. It is sometimes said that irony and symbol work together, and it may be that ultimately they do. But surely at first, and insofar as we can consider artistic method at all, irony and symbol are mutually exclusive. With symbol go allegory, icon, music, rite and myth.

Irony is different from all these, for it is tied to realism from the first: it can function, that is, only when we are convinced of the validity of both 'the one thing' and 'the other.' Coriolanus must be so real to us that we *know* his determination to be gentle, and that we *know* he cannot be so. The juxtaposition destroys unity, destroys simplicity, and since we must draw off to correlate incongruities, irony is 'detachment.' Detachment, however, need not suggest indifference; in fact, sympathetic involvement, or charity even, is the more likely concomitant of artistic irony. For to see a man labouring under a limited view of things is to understand that man's condition the better, and to understand is at least to tolerate, if not to pity and forgive. By his realism the artist maintains our sense of fellow-feeling with his characters, so that although the *view* may be from the top of whatever hierarchy we can conceive of, we nevertheless know that our actual *position* is at the bottom along with everybody else, and the pity follows as an extension of self-pity.

The ironist destroys unity, or the absolute, and sets up multiplicity, or the relative. By destroying simplistic illusions he inculcates newer, less simple ideas that are more answerable to 'the way things are.' He insists on paradox, and deflates monisms. We see on his stage people acting with a sense of free will, and he shows us the inexorable chain of cause and effect. Or, if the chain is conspicuous, he reminds us how we are like these people; we, like them, 'know' the decisions are ours to make. He deflates our pretentions to rationality and insists on the perverse and the absurd. He deflates our pride in institutions, playing on the discrepancy between the man and his office. He deflates 'romantic' ideas of love by countering with actual physical and emotional exigencies.

He shows men tugged about by conflicts of self-interest and social interest, by conflicts of two self-interests, or even two social interests and discovers them as mixed, confused, and perverse. But he does not blink the fact that there are good men and noble actions. In fact, the ironist may blink no fact available to him: the condition of irony must be a certain free play of mind. If he denies himself the right to consider some facet of life that is known to him, his work is invalidated by that denial. It is his business to make convention serve his sense of the truth. If the facets of 'reality' do not strike us as real, the irony loses its distinction.

Irony has a special affinity for the drama, because ironic juxtaposition is a display and therefore in itself implies stage and spectators. The ironic art of juxtaposition does not necessarily arrive at conclusions, and neither does the drama, for the essential is in the presentation of characters and actions, and conclusions tend to be simplistic. Hence it is that our first best theory in English of irony as something more than a figure of speech—Thirlwall's essay on Sophocles—came out of a consideration of the drama. Certainly the concept of dramatic irony has aided immeasurably in the understanding of the genre, and it seems to promise a yet unexploited usefulness in the theory of fiction. The nub of dramatic irony consists in the spectators' knowing more than the actors, and its most conspicuous manifestation is the speech or action with double or multiple meaning. Ironic drama, then, depends on having no mysteries—the more we know, the more possibilities for irony. So it is that the *ficta nota* is a positive advantage. Altogether, the drama is a particularly dynamic means of demonstrating the contrarieties of reality, and by the demonstration enjoins the ironic view.

The story-teller must forego some of the advantages of dramatic irony: he may lose his reader at any time to the telephone, to sleep, to work, or to a visitor from Porlock. He must forego the sense of occasion that the theatre offers, and the intensity of focus. But he can nevertheless appropriate many elements of the theatre. Certainly he can use dialogue, and whenever there is dialogue there is the possibility to exploit dramatic irony. He can present his characters as flesh and blood, and—if he is good—they can be even more real than actors because there is no 'acting.' Because he can record thought as well as behaviour, there is a whole special range of irony available to him in the incongruities between thought and action. He can use 'dramatic' situations, where conflicts come into crisis. And he can keep the reader informed of all, making no mystery; so that we are superior and partake of the ironic vantage point.

Furthermore, non-dramatic literature has some special advantages even in irony. It has the advantage of the singer or narrator who is free to exploit a relationship to his material on the one hand and to his reader on the other. The drama suffers from the lack of this, and compensates by various devices—chorus, or commentator, or Stage Manager as persona. It is the commentator-narrator who best establishes and maintains ironic detachment, which can be taken as another name for 'aesthetic distance.' In a sense the story-teller is always ironic insofar as the story is art; the artist is superior to his material as the man who narrates a robbery to the police is not. Or the poet even in a *cri de coeur* is more ironic than the man who screams with pain.

But the story-teller who is especially ironic excels in manipulating those two relationships—with his subject matter and with his reader. His 'saying one thing and meaning another' requires a very special relationship of understanding from his reader or of course the 'meaning' will fail. The relationship implies a common ground of superiority in knowledge. It functions best if he is our friend, more than a mere presence or acquaintance. He does well to convince us of his honesty, or else we cannot be intimate or take his reports in good faith. It is part of his art to keep us aware of his presence, for it is our pleasure and profit to stand with him and share his wise detachment—if he has it—his laughter, his tolerance, his morality.

Certainly Trollope exemplifies this authorial friendship. By presenting his ambivalent *cases* he invites us to share the double view, from his ironic vantage point. Kenneth Burke calls irony a dialectic: *The Warden case*, in this sense, presents two very *speaking* arguments: Mr. Harding's is eloquent, and so is John Bold's. Neither can be dismissed; they must be correlated. And so by the dialectic, we arrive—still in Burke's terms—at the *perspective of perspectives*, the new ironic overview.[2] Trollope refuses to make a mystery, because he wants us to know as much as possible.[3] Thomas Mann considers that the novel is now our supreme art form because of this irony. The novel is the Apollonian art—Apollo 'der Gott der Distanz, der Objectivität, der Gott der Ironie. Objectivität ist Ironie'—'Apollo, the god of distance, of objectivity, the god of irony. Objectivity is irony.' The novel is *criticism*, in comparison to the naïveté of primitive art: it is 'Schöpferisches Bewusstein zum unbewussten Schaffen.'[4] Trollope's novels are full of this awareness, this criticism, of behaviour, of social institutions, of literary institutions including the novel itself.

To try to define is to try to limit, but ironic art is by nature unlimited. There is no visible end to the kinds of ambivalence to be explored. We speak of ambi-valences, and ambi-

guities, and we speak of discrepancies in pairs; I think we do
this only because we can think better in terms of two than in
terms of multiples. Like the machines, our minds work well
on a binary system. But in practice, ironic art can help us
work in multiples, it can stretch our understanding farther
than any theory allows for. If we remember how close *irony*
is in practice to *humour*, and how little we have been able to
do in analysing *humour*, we realise that we are hardly up to
any definitive theory. When Louis Cazamian writes of
Chaucer's *humour*, he does about as well as can be done,
perhaps; especially well because he is himself the outside
observer of the particularly English phase of this process.
And Trollope as ironic story-teller has very much in common
with Chaucer. Chaucer's humour is

> the very spirit of relativity, the diversity, the unreasonable-
> ness of things. A pragmatist would say that the philosophy
> of humour was pluralistic; and indeed it is made up of the
> acceptance of the stubborn contradictions which our en-
> deavours in all fields fail to eradicate, and there is no greater
> enemy to humour than the passion of unity.

Its 'natural outcome' is, he says,

> a tolerance, a readiness to understand, almost to sympathise;
> a broad genial humanity, if not necessarily, as has often been
> said, a tenderness and a love.
>   Chaucer, from the mental watch-tower whence he surveys
> the world of his time, has taken in all the varieties and the
> absurdities; he has noted the discrepancies of character, the
> perverse individualities of creatures, the shiftings of ap-
> pearance. His intelligence is reconciled with the relativity of
> things; and his eye quietly looks for the contrast, the opposi-
> tion, the other side . . .; to all the unaccountable habits of
> men and of fate, he responds with the suppleness of mind
> which no single formula has enslaved; and as his reaction is
> free and easy, it is immune from the pain of disappointed
> expectations or jarred principles.

Then Cazamian does speak of irony, 'the irony that accepts
and forgives,' and he says:

The instinct of relativity which is the soul of humour is reflected in its method; it will say one thing, and mean another thing; or rather it will bring out more forcibly what it does not actually say, adding point to a suggestion by its very indirectness. Just as its matter lies in contrasts, its manner is an inversion, a transposition.[5]

We all know well enough that Trollope's humour is of the most telling importance, but we are rather helpless to explain it. Its common ground with irony is an area where we can understand it a little, perhaps. Tragic irony is easier to anatomise than comic irony, but as Aristodemus remembered hearing just before he fell asleep, Socrates was saying the genius of comedy was really the same as that of tragedy. The others were all 'compelled to assent, being sleepy, and not quite understanding his meaning.'

There is a late novel of Trollope's that in its Apollonian critical way suggests the significance of the 'genius of comedy.' It is *Ayala's Angel*, just a novel of courtship, showing some inheritance from Jane Austen's *Sense and Sensibility*. Yet this is a rich and benign work, with many beautiful complications; its tracing and contrasting of courtships is finally a celebration of the richness of life. Ayala is the nineteen-year-old daughter of an artist, who is just dead when the novel starts, but present in spirit as a sense of the values of liberal culture. She is consigned to two guardian households one after the other, one wealthy Philistine and the other scrape-and-save Philistine. She nurses an ideal: she will, she determines, never fall in love with anyone but the Angel of Light who may come at last and deliver her. He is quite transcendental, rather like Werther, and rather like Shelley. He is a poet, of course. Ayala suffers in alien Philistia, and grows intellectually and emotionally, steadfast to her ideal of the Angel, courageous to the point of determining to keep herself for him even if he should never come. Meantime there is some comfort in the company of Colonel Jonathan Stubbs, who is not at all like Shelley. His name is absurdly graceless; he is ugly, with a very large mouth and red face, and red bristles for hair. Although he is urbane and intellectually inclined and moves in the cultivated circles where Ayala's father had lived, he does not write poetry. He has done something or other very brave and useful to his country. But there is something else about him of great importance: he has a glorious, abounding, enchanting, outrageously inventive wit. He is really 'the Genius of Comedy,' without which, Trollope says in quiet understatement, 'life would be very dull' (xvi). Trollope presents Ayala's gradual discovery that this man whose company is the most delightful imaginable is in fact her true Angel of Light, in his untranscendental blessed physical actuality, her true deliverer.

There is an ironic deflation of a romantic ideal here, and something far more satisfactory to take its place. The novel is a story of growing-up, which someone said is in itself a dialectical process; and the reading of the novel is the dialectical process of irony. Life is *not* dull; and Trollope in league with the Genius of Comedy shows that it is not. The novels themselves, too, in taking us 'out of dead intellectuality into moral perception,' take us out of dullness into engagement. And perhaps finally they teach us to be less absurd.

NOTES

[1]Paris, Libraries Félix Alcan, 1909, p. 163.

[2]*A Grammar of Motives*, p. 503.

[3]Trollope's most important statement of the no-mysteries principle is *Barchester Towers*, xv; here he is especially clear on the value of dramatic irony, even referring to Plautus. Some of his other statements of the principle are: *The Bertrams*, xiii; *The Eustace Diamonds*, xlviii and lii; *Marion Fay*, xxxi; *Dr. Wortle's School*, iii. And *Dr. Thorne* is a conspicuous case; here for once, he took over a conventional 'plot' (it was his brother Tom's idea), but he refuses us the conventional treatment. *We* know all about the mystery of Mary's birth at the beginning.

[4]'Die Kunst des Romans' (Lecture at Princeton, 1939) in *Altes und Neues: Kleine Prosa aus fünf Jahrzehnten*. Frankfurt-am-Main, S. Fischer, 1953, pp. 387–401.

[5]*The Development of English Humour*. New York, Macmillan, 1930, pp. 102–105.

INDEX

INDEX